# Killer
# Broadband

"Eye Testing" and Other Government Surveillances

Dillon Joseph Woods

# DEDICATION

This book is dedicated to all the innocent people who have suffered at the hands of corrupt and unscrupulous government agents and agencies.

# CONTENTS

# ACKNOWLEDGMENTS

ChatGPT is changing the way humans write their books, articles, and other writing projects. It's a new technology that acts like a free research assistant that gets the job done in five seconds. Assuming this new technology will increase the knowledge, accurateness, and truthfulness of information it shares... Thanks must go to those humans who helped make ChatGPT possible.

# 1 INTRODUCTION

Getting broadband internet into rural communities throughout the United States is a high priority for many politicians making promises for the upcoming elections. *"Some 42 million Americans have no access to broadband, according to Broadband Now, a data technology company. In Louisiana, 1.7 million people, more than a third of the state's population, have this critical need."* ([https://www.pbs.org/newshour/nation/more-than-1-in-3-louisiana-residents-dont-have-high-speed-internet-the-state-has-a-plan-to-change-that](https://www.pbs.org/newshour/nation/more-than-1-in-3-louisiana-residents-dont-have-high-speed-internet-the-state-has-a-plan-to-change-that)).

ChatGPT Bard (2023) was able to quickly show me recent headlines about this broadband issue: *"Here are some recent news headlines from around the country regarding the government's priority of bringing broadband to the entire country:*

*Biden administration announces $2.8 billion in funding to expand broadband access. (CNBC) www.cnet.com*

*FCC unveils new map of broadband availability in the United States. (Federal Communications Commission) broadband.colorado.gov*

*State governments are taking steps to bridge the digital divide. (National Conference of State Legislatures) www.schoolnetindia.com*

*The private sector is also investing in broadband expansion. (The Wall Street Journal) www.govtech.com*

*Broadband access is essential for economic growth and social equity. (Brookings Institution) www.investopedia.com*

*These headlines reflect the growing recognition that broadband access is essential for economic growth, social equity, and national security. The government, the private sector, and communities are working together to bridge the digital divide and ensure that everyone has access to the internet."*

I suspect that some politician's passion to make this happen as quickly as possible has less to do with care for the community and the economy than it does with personal financial opportunity and their personal financial prosperity. Getting broadband into every community is an avenue for some of these politicians to make large amounts of money for their own personal treasury accounts. Let me explain…

The United States government (or maybe it is better said: some people who work as agents for the United States government) have embarked on an extremely profitable and highly unethical, and often deceitful path of "eye testing" citizens through computers and televisions without the citizen's knowledge or consent. This "eye testing" project can't be done efficiently unless everyone has access to broadband. You heard that right: through the cameras on computers and televisions, scores of government agents are watching what, exactly, a person's eyes are focused on when you look at a movie, picture or video that is on your screen.

How I came to be aware of this program and examples of what they are doing, specifically, are in this book. I'm writing this book because what they are doing with this kind of testing is making them unbelievably rich (we're talking hundreds of billions of dollars rich) via unbelievably deceitful, unethical methods and motives. Americans need to be warned about how these unethical government agents are using taxpayer money against American citizens. Failing these tests can bring grave consequences to some citizens – including death.

The methods and motives of these government agents are complex and intertwined - as one might expect from Harvard business graduates and Harvard trained attorneys, such as the ones that I have encountered and done battle with over this issue for many years. There is a lot of evidence that points to fact that some of these government agents are sociopaths and psychopaths with fancy Harvard degrees. I'll do what I can to unravel and explain what I have experienced and come to witness for myself on this issue of the government program on "eye testing" and other government surveillances.

## MONEY, THE ROOT MOTIVATION

First, let's start from the beginning of what motivates these government agents: money. The government pays agents large sums of money to find and kill threats to national security. What defines a "threat to national security" depends on who is President of the United States and what administration you look at.

Some people say that who is President of the United States does not matter to an average American. However, when you look at an issue like national security, it clearly does matter because what an administration declares on an issue like this has ramifications even in the smallest towns in America.

As ChatGPT Bard (2023) says, *"The phrase "threat to national security" was used broadly during the George W. Bush administration, encompassing a wide range of individuals and activities deemed to pose a risk to the United States. This expansive definition was applied not only to individuals engaged in terrorism or espionage, but also to those who committed nonviolent offenses, such as immigration violations or protest activities.*

*The use of the term "threat to national security" in this context was criticized by some who argued that it was being used too loosely to justify the infringement of civil liberties. They contended that the government was overreaching in its definition of what constituted a threat, and that this was leading to the erosion of fundamental rights.*

*Despite these criticisms, the Bush administration maintained its expansive definition of "threat to national security," arguing that it was necessary to protect the country from potential threats. The administration's approach to national security was shaped by the events of September 11, and it reflected a belief that the government needed to take a more proactive approach to identifying and preventing potential threats.*

*The question of whether or not the Bush administration's definition of "threat to national security" is still in effect today is a complex one. While the Obama administration made some changes to the way in which the government handles national security threats, it also continued to use some of the same broad measures that were employed during the Bush era. Ultimately, the answer to this question depends on how one defines the term "threat to national security." If one takes a narrow view of the term, then it could be argued that the Bush administration's definition is no longer in effect. However, if one takes a broader view of the term, then it could be argued that some elements of the Bush administration's approach to national security are still in place today.*

*The debate over the definition of 'threat to national security' is likely to continue for many years to come. As the United States faces new and evolving threats, the government will need to carefully consider how to define and address these threats while also protecting the rights of its citizens."*

What Bard does not tell you is that one reason this 'national security' debate will continue for many years is because of the "powers and principalities" that profit large amounts of money from projects like this 'eye testing' scam that I'm describing in this book. They will drag this debate on 'national security' out as long as they can – solely to continue profiteering. The longer they can drag this out, the more billions of dollars they will make. Greed is at the root of dragging this issue out.

## COMMUNITY POLICING – IF YOU SEE SOMETHING, SAY SOMETHING

During the George W. Bush administration, it was decided by someone that anyone who broke any law (even small, insignificant laws) could be considered a terrorist and a threat to national security. Billboards and posters went up all over America recruiting people to be spies in their local community. "If you see something, say something" became a moto you heard on TVs, radios, sports competitions, schools and in airports throughout the country. It became common for average citizens to look for terrorists and criminals in their community.

According to ChatGPT, *"The Citizen Corps was a U.S. government initiative created to encourage community involvement in emergency preparedness, response, and public safety initiatives. It was established in the aftermath of the September 11, 2001, terrorist attacks as part of the USA Freedom Corps, an effort to engage citizens in service and volunteering to address various national challenges.*

*The primary goal of Citizen Corps was to promote grassroots participation in bolstering community resilience against various emergencies, including natural disasters, terrorist threats, and other hazards. This initiative sought to educate and train citizens in emergency response, preparedness, and mitigation strategies.*

*Within the broader framework of Citizen Corps, the Neighborhood Watch program played a crucial role. Neighborhood Watch is a community-based crime prevention program that encourages residents to work together and with local law enforcement to keep their neighborhoods safe by being vigilant, reporting suspicious activities, and implementing crime prevention measures.*

*The Citizen Corps initiative encompassed several programs and campaigns, including:*

**Community Emergency Response Teams** *(CERT): CERT trained volunteers to assist first responders during emergencies, providing immediate assistance to victims, organizing spontaneous volunteers, and performing light search and rescue operations.*

**Volunteers in Police Service** *(VIPS): VIPS aimed to enhance the capacity of law enforcement agencies by recruiting and utilizing volunteers to support various police department initiatives, such as administrative tasks, crime prevention programs, and community outreach efforts.*

**Medical Reserve Corps** *(MRC): MRC engaged medical and public health professionals, as well as community volunteers, to respond to public health emergencies, assist in disaster relief efforts, and promote community health initiatives.*

**Fire Corps**: *Fire Corps focused on recruiting and training community members to support local fire departments and emergency services through non-emergency tasks, such as fire safety education, fundraising, and administrative assistance.*

*Overall, the Citizen Corps initiative aimed to empower individuals and communities to take an active role in enhancing public safety, emergency preparedness, and response capabilities, fostering a sense of civic responsibility and community resilience in the face of various threats and challenges."*

These programs and programs like them were in every town – large and small – in America. This greatly aided the government agents who were secretly making money from finding and killing "terrorists" and "criminals" who were "threats to national security." So, if an agent could find someone breaking any law, they could put that person on a watch list and work on setting them up, framing them. This "eye testing" program is part of the "framing" machine the Checchi's have created. And like Santa Clause, these government agents began extensive lists on millions of American citizens of every age (even high school and college students) and they were checking their lists twice to find out who was being naughty and nice.

Allegedly, not one family was more successful at these scams against the American people than the CIA Checchi family. Did they catch and kill real, mean bad guys? You bet they did. Did they catch and kill completely innocent people whose only fault was being gullible, naïve, and easy to manipulate into Checchi-orchestrated scams? You bet they did. In the beginning of their careers as government agents, I suspect the Checchi's caught and killed genuine bad guys – genuine threats to America's national security.

But as they came to see how easy it was to set up people and frame people they didn't like as criminals (for example, some of these Checchi cult leaders are very racist. They don't like black people, Jewish people, gay people, devout Christians, Catholics, or devout Muslims) they began to shift their priority to making large amounts of money. They made large amounts of money by playing manipulative games with naïve, gullible people. They secretly made hundreds of billions of dollars killing people they just didn't agree with or like. Soon, their full-time job became playing games with and tricking gullible people and the families & friends of these gullible people. From what I have seen for myself over the last twenty years of knowing this CIA family, this became the Checchi's main bread and butter. "Unethical" doesn't even begin to explain the level of corruption I have witnessed with this CIA Checchi family cult. They rarely act in good faith and their investigations are top heavy with extreme bias, tremendous manipulation, and pure fraud – such as photoshopped photos, "deep fake" videos and "witnesses" who are paid $$$ to lie.

The CIA Checchi cult leaders call me a 'traitor' for exposing their crimes and writing books detailing their crimes against the American people and their crimes against humanity. This is more proof that they have started their own country and have their own set of laws.

Under American law, the Constitution defines what a traitor is. In Article III, Section 3. It states: "*Treason against the United States shall consist only in levying War against them, or in adhering to their Enemies, giving them Aid and Comfort. No Person shall be convicted of Treason unless on the Testimony of two Witnesses to the same overt Act, or on Confession in open Court.*" Being a traitor is connected to war. Only Congress can declare war – not the CIA, not the military, not a person in the CIA and not the CIA Checchi family. The CIA Checchi family has declared war on secret societies and this war has gone on for over fifty years – millions of people have been secretly killed. This prolonged war has been a massive mistake on the part of the CIA Checchi family cult. As it says in the *Art of War* by Master S. Tzu,

# *"When you do battle, even if you are winning, if you continue for a long time, it will dull your forces and blunt your edge; if you besiege a citadel, your strength will be exhausted. If you keep your armies out in the field for a long time, your supplies will be insufficient."*

Like those who are part of the ill-informed "sovereign citizen" movement, the CIA Checchi family cult leaders believe they are above the laws of ordinary American citizens. When they claim journalists who report the truth about them are 'traitors' they show they have their own set of laws which establishes they have their own country and their own laws. Ironically, they have built their own country on American citizen's taxpayer dollars.

When President Donald Trump said on January 6, 2021, *"If you don't fight like hell, you're not going to have a country anymore."* That's what he was talking about. He wasn't talking about the United States of America as a country. He's talking about the country that the CIA Checchi family cult has created for itself – of which Trump has been a prominent leader for decades. The cult leaders knew that once Trump was out of power as president, many people would work to shut down the CIA Checchi family cult because it had become obvious that they were too powerful, too secretive, too un-American, and too dangerous for innocent Americans. While Trump was president, the CIA Checchi family cult made great progress because they could do whatever they wanted to do. They did many calculated, illegal things to solidify their power, make billions of dollars and improve their control over military and political leaders. They depended on frequent, secret presidential pardons from President Trump to clean up the mess they made doing illegal things to make money and increase their power base.

I'm not sure how much money a government agent makes from killing a threat to national security, but I'm certain it's a lot of money per person. Over many decades, the CIA Checchi family has created a machine that manipulates gullible citizens, frames them, and then kills them – reaping billions. All of this has been done in mystery because CIA people are cloaked with secrecy.

People like the CIA Checchi family (with whom I have been in a court battle from 2020 – 2023) have been prolific abusers of this government system, secretly reaping hundreds of billions of dollars for themselves (adding up to trillions over several decades). This kind of abuse and exploitation of the system needs to be exposed and stopped, hence I decided to write this book.

If I understand correctly, before a government agent can legally kill someone, they must compile evidence that the person was a threat to national security, a threat to the community. If enough "evidence" and "data" was collected on a person which showed this person was bad for society and a 'threat to national security,' that person can be put on a kill list. This could include people who commit crimes like property crimes (burglary, theft, motor vehicle theft, arson, and vandalism), drug crimes (including Driving Under the Influence of drugs or alcohol), white collar crimes (fraud, embezzlement, identity theft, and money laundering), violent crimes /murders (homicide, assault, robbery, and domestic violence), sexual deviants/rapists, cybercrimes, disturbing the peace crimes, weapons crimes, and hate crimes against people based on their race, sexual orientation, religion, ethnicity, etc.

Once the government agent establishes that someone is worthy of being put on a kill list, the next issue is how to kill that person. A

Checchi cult leader once bragged to me that *"we have a thousand ways to kill someone."* This is done by a variety of means in today's modern world. One option they like using is via a doctor or dentist who would secretly inject a deadly disease into the person when they think they are getting a flu shot or Novocain. Another favorite method is more aggressive: they arrange an "accident" in which the person gets killed.

For example, California is among the deadliest states for male crash victims, *"Men are more likely to be killed in a car crash than women in all 50 states, a new study has found, and California is listed among the top 10 deadliest states for male crash victims… California placed eighth on the list with a ratio of just over four male crash deaths for every one female, research shows, meaning that men are four times more likely to die in a collision than women in California. Men in California and Florida are exactly 4.03 times more likely to be killed in a car crash than their female counterparts in those states, the study found. Each state ranked first and second in total crash fatalities, with 10,578 and 9,472 respectively. According to the California Office of Traffic Safety, traffic deaths increased approximately 7.6 percent from 2020 to 2021."* (https://www.yahoo.com/news/california-among-deadliest-states-male-175442918.html). There is no doubt that some of these deaths were orchestrated murders made to look like "accidents" because that's how CIA Checchi family government agents operate.

## GARBAGE SCIENCE, MANIPULATED DATA

The CIA Checchi family "data" collected via their unscientific, manipulated "eye testing" on computer and television is pure garbage science. For example, the Checchi's orchestrated "butt" and "breast" games via various media (movies, TV shows, commercials, video games, etc.) is constant Checchi nonsense that has been going on for a long time. Below are more details regarding this CIA Checchi family nonsense.

Since the CIA Checchi family is based in California, they control Hollywood and all companies that make movies. It is almost impossible to find a movie that is not filled with unfair, biased and manipulated scenes that are designed to make a person's eye focus on someone's butt, breasts, or other body parts the Checchi's deem inappropriate or signs of being a "deviant" or "predator." The massive amount of manipulation in movies is so overwhelming, this would be a very large book if I were to document all the examples of their manipulated nonsense that I have seen just in the last few years.

But this kind of manipulation is not just in movies, TV shows or commercials. The CIA Checchi cult leaders have constantly manipulated things to appear on my social media as they attempted to frame me. For example, I have a ghost in my Instagram feed. Things like this video appear frequently, even though I'm not subscribed to the channels that upload the videos. Here's a butt snippet video they put up recently on my Instagram channel:

https://www.instagram.com/reel/CwbblgtJL_S/?utm_source=ig_web_copy_link

A screen shot of the video:

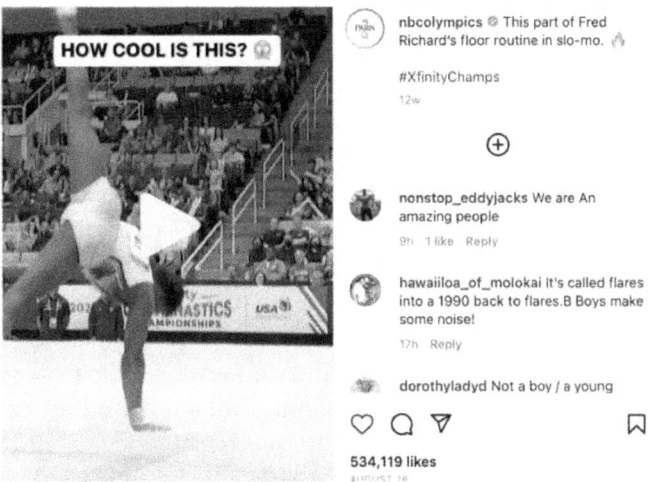

Below is a small sampling of things that have come on my computer as they try to frame me as a sick fetish person focused on butts and breasts. What they do in this regard is complete nonsense and more CIA Checchi family manipulation. They are not just doing this to me, they are doing this to literally thousands and thousands of Americans on Facebook, Twitter, Instagram, and other social media. They have a machine of entrapment, manipulation and undue influence that reaps for them hundreds of billions of dollars.

## SEEING IS BELIEVING

In this lecture that was given at Stanford University (link below), "SEEING IS BELIEVING," the science behind visual sight and neural brain connections the teacher explains in detail how brains work. "Brain wiring" is possible through repeated visual cues. How this relates to the CIA's program of "eye testing," "mind control," and "brain washing" is that if you can get someone to look at something they normally would not look at enough times, you can train them to look at these things all the time. It's a form of CIA brainwashing and mind control. When you brain wash someone, you can influence and control their behavior.

This science says that you can create patterns of connections: "cells that fire together, wire together" is the phrase that is used in the video at the link (39 minutes 57 seconds) to describe this process of brain wiring. So, the bottom line is: as the CIA Checchi family inundate someone with the same constant visual stimuli (an arrow pointing at a person's breasts or butt, for example or a female with large breasts wearing a t-shirt with words to read in the area of the breasts), you can eventually make them look at a person's breasts or butt without the arrow pointing or the words on a t-shirt being present. It's a way to train or brainwash "hard wired" someone's behavior.

This is why it is said that "the CIA can turn anyone into any kind of criminal." In less extreme terms, the CIA can make anyone look at anything on their computer or television, given enough time to train their brain to "auto dial." The Checchi's are doing this brain washing nonsense to thousands and thousands of naïve, gullible citizens in order to make money claiming they are finding "threats to national security," "predators" or "perverts." These are tricks of psychological manipulation which the CIA Checchi family has become famous for. THEY MUST BE STOPPED FROM DOING THIS.

### "SEEING IS BELIEVING"
STANFORD LECTURE, FEBRUARY 2, 2010.
https://www.youtube.com/watch?v=21_VWHKcNlg&list=PLt L-ABqnN-k_9i4ni2XxBADCImfkKw5g&index=654

Carla Shatz, professor of biology and neurobiology at the Stanford School of Medicine, discusses the visual processes of the brain, while Mark Blumenkranz, professor of opthalmology at Stanford Medical Center, focuses on developments in ophthalmological treatment.

Stanford Mini Med School is a series arranged and directed by Stanford's School of Medicine and presented by the Stanford Continuing Studies program. Featuring more than thirty distinguished, faculty, scientists and physicians from Stanford's medical school, the series offers students a dynamic introduction to the world of human biology, health and disease, and the groundbreaking changes taking place in medical research and health care.

Stanford University: http://www.stanford.edu/

## PHOTOGRAPH TRICKS

One of the "tricks" the CIA Checchi family cult leaders have used on me: the CIA Checchi cult leaders play two games with photographs to get someone to look at a woman's breasts.

1. They constantly have commercials for bras pop up on my computer as I watch programs on YouTube.

2. They put a t-shirt with words or a sentence on the front of the shirt, with a female who has large breasts. As you read the t-shirt, you are guilty of sexualizing the woman because you are also simultaneously staring at her breasts while you read the t-shirt. This is the kind of nonsense "eye testing" scam that the CIA Checchi family orchestrates against American's – our tax dollars hard at work.

The CIA is under the umbrella of the military. Therefore, the CIA Checchi family is under the umbrella of the military. The military and the CIA allow this nonsense "eye testing" to go on as they attack and manufacture this "data" on American citizens using computers and televisions with hidden cameras. There is a case to be made that these hidden cameras violate the Fourth Amendment.

As ChatGPT (2023) says, *"The Fourth Amendment of the United States Constitution protects individuals from unreasonable searches and seizures by the government and requires warrants to be supported by probable cause when searches or seizures are conducted. The use of hidden cameras on computers and televisions by either the government or private entities could potentially implicate Fourth Amendment concerns in certain situations:*

***Government Surveillance:*** *If the government installs hidden cameras on computers or televisions without a proper warrant or probable cause, it could be considered an unreasonable search and violation of privacy rights guaranteed by the Fourth Amendment. This is particularly relevant if the surveillance intrudes into areas where individuals have a reasonable expectation of privacy, such as inside their homes.*

***Private Entity Intrusion:*** *If a private entity, such as a hacker or a company, installs hidden cameras on devices without the user's consent and monitors* *individuals without their knowledge, it may not directly implicate the Fourth Amendment. However, it can still violate privacy laws or regulations, depending on the circumstances and jurisdiction.*

*In both cases, the key factors that determine Fourth Amendment violations include whether there is a reasonable expectation of privacy, whether a warrant was obtained (if required), and whether the surveillance was conducted in a manner that intrudes upon an individual's reasonable expectation of privacy.*

*Courts assess these situations on a case-by-case basis, considering factors such as the nature of the intrusion, the location of the surveillance, the individual's reasonable expectation of privacy, and the government's or private entity's justification for the surveillance. If the use of hidden cameras on computers or televisions infringes upon an individual's reasonable expectation of privacy without proper legal authorization, it could potentially be considered a violation of the Fourth Amendment."*

I was once in a conversation with one of the CIA Checchi family cult leaders about hidden cameras. He admitted to wide use of hidden cameras in their operations. He said, *"just because the video footage is not admissible in court, it doesn't mean we won't do it just to find out what is really going on."* How did government agents ever get to this kind of mentality from the Fourth Amendment of the Constitution which protects individuals against unreasonable searches and seizures? This Amendment has been interpreted by the Supreme Court to include a reasonable expectation of privacy in various contexts, such as the home, personal belongings, and electronic communications.

I once faced government retribution after writing a letter to Apple's CEO asking for a MacBook Pro laptop that was not wired with spy gadgets – including hidden cameras on the computer that violate the Fourth Amendment in the American Constitution. I should not be the one punished for safeguarding my constitutional rights on my computer. The CIA Checchi family or the military/CIA should be fined money for violating the rights of American citizens as outlined in the Fourth Amendment. Each citizen whose rights have been violated should be compensated with this money. The idea that *"just because the video footage is not admissible in court, it doesn't mean we won't do it just to find out what is really going on,"* contradicts the principles of America's constitution and the right to privacy.

# 2 APPLE+

Apple+ has a very ambitious and large section of movies and shows they offer to people who have Apple devices. They even offer a free 7-day subscription for each of their channels. Many of these shows and movies have been craftily created by the CIA Checchi family cult leaders. These cult leaders are the most dangerous terrorist network in the world, and they use movies and TV shows to train and communicate with their vast network of 500+ million spies worldwide. They also use these shows and movies to set people up and, in the process, the CIA Checchi cult leaders make hundreds of billions of dollars for their own financial interests.

In this chapter, I explain in detail how just one show (*Banshee*) helped them reap a massive financial wind fall. Usually, the movies and shows that the Checchi's get involved in have their messages sprinkled throughout the script. In *Banshee* the entire show is filled with messages, brain washing tricks, and every character is telling aspects of Checchi cult leaders. I've rarely seen a show so filled with multi-tasking aspects for their varied cult members and information for potential recruits of the cult.

What I write here is not written to say anything bad about the company Apple or the leadership that makes and distributes movies, TV shows, and Apple technology products. These prolific, creative, and wealthy companies have been hijacked, infiltrated, and used by the CIA Checchi family cult leaders for their own financial profit and manipulative purposes.

It is possible that companies such as Apple and the production companies that make movies and TV shows are oblivious to being hijacked and used for purposes these companies are unaware of and consciously uninvolved in.

The art of infiltration is one thing. The art of secretly making billions of dollars from these infiltrations is another. The CIA Checchi family cult leaders are unmatched in their ability to infiltrate and make outrageous sums of money from these infiltrations. However, their constant unethical behavior and disregard for laws makes them not only dangerous to deal with, but they have become a clear threat to the national interests and national security of the United States of America. Innocent American citizens are in danger. This book is written as a warning to help people understand how the leaders of this CIA Checchi family cult operate their manipulative, dishonest and prolifically dangerous surveillance "eye testing" programs.

One of the most polished and dangerous shows that I found on Apple+ is called, *Banshee* (which can be found on Cinemax). In typical 'late bloomer' fashion, I discovered the show ten years after it first aired in 2013. *"Banshee originally aired on the Cinemax network from January 11, 2013, to May 20, 2016, over four seasons, comprising a total of 38 episodes."* (https://en.wikipedia.org/wiki/Banshee_TV_series). One of the most relevant quotes from the show is from season 4, episode 5 – 'Words to live by:' *"You know what they say, just cause you're paranoid, don't mean they ain't all out to get you."* Truer words have never been spoken when it comes to the CIA Checchi family terrorist cult.

This show serves as a recruiting tool for their cult and a training tool for those already part of the cult: police, criminals, teens, and more. I've seen many of the Checchi's shows and movies over the years and *Banshee* is an example of how polished, multi-faceted, multi-dimensional, and multi-tasking their productions have become. All this with great writing, excellent plot creation, excellent camera work and very creative editing. The actors in *Banshee* are also very good at their craft.

Why would CIA people create such provocative shows and movies? This show serves many purposes for the CIA Checchi family: it is training for all the Checchi's "fake cops" around the country (the Checchi's infiltrate police stations and court rooms all over the United States and sabotage the rule of law for their own greedy purposes). *Banshee* is also training for their army of criminals throughout the world and much, much more.

The Checchi's make sure the program gives classes on how to get away with various crimes, using technology. *Banshee* is a class on the do's and don'ts of how to execute various crimes.

To attract the military crowd, they even include the military in a few episodes and reveal a few military secrets. They also tell people how to evade various alarms that are found in businesses. They even have a transgender character, who is often seen in drag – he's a fighter, commits prolific cybercrimes and is one of the main characters in every episode.

The show offers an abundance of teenage and adult nudity and an abundance of long, drawn-out violence. The show also serves as a training tool and recruitment tool for young men who have a predisposition to fighting. The culture of fighting/hand to hand combat is glorified and part of every episode in *Banshee*.

One of the most dramatic "fight club" scenes is from season 3, episode 7 (5:00 minutes), where you see teens shouting support for one fighter or the other… while some others are caught up in sexualizing each other/making out and can't be bothered to watch the fight.

The Checchi's are the original promoters of the "fight club" genre. The CIA Checchi family cult leaders are raising an army of young men and women to hijack American democracy. They need young men who can fight or willing to be trained to fight when their violent revolution against American democracy starts (the CIA Checchi cult leaders were the group that organized and orchestrated the insurrection at the Capitol in Washington, D.C. on January 6, 2021. This was a dress rehearsal for what they plan to do at some point in the future, if they are not permanently stopped.). Their aggressive recruitment of fighters starts in high schools and colleges throughout the country. If you've noticed an increase in teens being in the news for fighting and other violent crimes, it's not your imagination that this is a growing problem. It's being deliberately encouraged and orchestrated by the CIA Checchi family terrorist cult leaders to facilitate the chaos and mayhem they are planning for America and throughout the world.

In this *Banshee* show, they even have violence interspersed with more violence – multiple violent scenes operating simultaneously in season 2 episode 2. Not only is the violence prolific and constant, but it's also got a particular sickness to some of it – termed "Banshee Violence" because it is so extreme and filmed / acted / edited with intensity, precision, and creativity. In typical CIA Checchi family terrorist style, they've created their own brand of aberrant violence.

They also do this with sex in season 3; There are a tremendous amount of open sex scenes that are also long and drawn out.

Through all this drama in *Banshee*, they take time to tie in a conservative religion (they pick on the Amish people in this show… but it could be Mormons, Catholics, Baptists, Evangelicals, Orthodox Jews, or devout Muslims. The religious issues they raise are found in many conservative religious groups, not just the Amish people). Religion is part of the entire series, and they frequently comment on religious people and the hypocrisy found with conservative religious communities. This show gives them the opportunity to comment on conservative religious people and show them to be heartless and out of touch.

During season 3, the writers even create "what if" or "if only" scenes and dream of a different life for various cast members – if only the original sheriff would not have died in season 1, episode 1. This was a very creative and unique choice to watch.

## TRICKS AND TRAPS IN *BANSHEE*

### TEEN AGE NUDITY TRAP

They warn people about nudity in the episodes, but they should be required to warn people about teenage nudity, as opposed to regular adult nudity. In places like season 2, episode 4 (38:05) they switch between teenage sex scenes and conservative Amish scenes. It may be legal to show a nude 18- or 19-year-old, but the consequences in real life according to unwritten CIA Checchi family law can be more severe and deadly. The Checchi's can accuse people who watch teen nudity of being into teenagers, which never goes over well – even if the teens are legally considered adults. In the world of the CIA Checchi family cult, there is a massive prohibition on adults having anything to do with anyone in their teenage years. So… shows like this should be required to explicitly warn people about teenage nudity in the beginning of a program. Teenage nudity is another common trick conceived by sophisticated Harvard scammers. Remember: they make billions of dollars coming up with these scams. So, new rules must be created to contain their nonsense and their scams involving any teens – even if they are legally seen as adults in society.

An example of a typical, cheesy butt shot can be seen season 2 episode 5, 34 minutes 28 seconds. Butt shots and boob shots (both clothed and naked) in this show are too numerous to list. The point of these shots (for the spies watching the viewer as the viewer watches the show) is get people to look at these private parts for at least two seconds - which gives these government agents ammunition to claim the viewer is depraved, perverted, immoral or a danger to the community. "His/Her viewing habits are a sign of deep inner dysfunction and perversion" is how they are trying to frame people. If they can acquire enough of this "evidence" it can be used to justify killing someone. It is very lucrative to kill someone in this category because these dysfunctional people are threat to a safe community. By killing someone on whom they have acquired a lot of this kind of "evidence," they are preventing a creep or predator from acting on what is obviously their inner most drives. This has similar theme to the movie, *Minority Report*, except this "eye testing" stuff is real life... not a movie.

In *Minority Report* political leaders in the future have created a "Precrime" police unit. They routinely arrest people for crimes they will commit in the future before they commit the crime.

I know this is true, because the CIA Checchi family pulled this nonsense on me when I was battling them in court. They tried to kill me several times and they used my computer "cookies" as evidence that I was a threat to national security based on my texting, email, and computer history. The only problem is, they forgot to mention to the judge that I let many Checchi spies use my computer and cell phone over the years. I was never guarded or suspicious of anyone asking to use my computer or cell phone. It turns out this was a mistake.

For example, some of these spies would often show me weird and ridiculously sick videos from various porn websites. It was done as a joke. I had no idea that a computer's "cookies are forever" and I was being fully and intensely manipulated by dangerous CIA Checchi spies who had been sent into my life to frame me and set me up. As the saying goes, "dance like no one is watching. But text, email and use your computer like it will all be read in open court one day."

I know I am not the only person they have done this to. They've framed and set up thousands and thousands of innocent people – possibly millions of people over five or six decades. Most of these people didn't end up in court with the CIA Checchi family because most people never figure out who is behind the curtain playing unethical spy games, framing them, and persecuting them.

The CIA Checchi family cult has an army of millions of spies who work hard at framing people day and night. In the process, the Checchi's have reaped hundreds of billions of dollars in reward money for "solving problems" before the people became a problem in the community. "Eye testing" is manipulated data and complete garbage science. The CIA Checchi family cult leaders are creating problems for people – problems that never would have existed if it weren't for the Checchi's manipulations and dishonesty.

VIOLENCE (V)

The violence in *Banshee* is constant and extreme. Violence and sex are the two most common scenes in this show. It would be very tedious and long to list all the violent scenes. So, I'll just list a few…

Season 1, episode 3 introduces the priority of betting on fights. UFC, MMA and any form of combat is something the CIA Checchi family is heavily involved in controlling and orchestrating in America and throughout the world. Most, if not all, of these fights are rigged and manipulated predetermining the winner. Nothing the Checchi family cult leaders are involved in is free from being manipulated and controlled. They control the referees, the sportscasters/sports analysts, the athletes, their managers & attorneys – the entire thing is an orchestrated production. Manipulated for the public's entertainment purposes and the Checchi's immense financial gain. They also get involved in the betting and gambling that goes on with these fights… raking in billions of dollars worldwide because they rig the fights.

With the introduction of the fighter for the special event, they waste no time giving a tip of the hat to military people: "*I want to give a semper fi to all my jar heads… you ready to see me whip some ass?*" Fighting is part of the military culture in the Marines. So, they make sure to include them as part of the audience they are attracting to watch this show. There are many military people who are part of the CIA Checchi family cult.

SEX & VIOLENCE (RAPE) (STRONG SEXUAL CONTENT) (SC)

The rape of women is a regular theme at various points throughout *Banshee*. The first time it appears in season 1, episode 3 (28:00) it is tied to the professional fighter. The target audience for *Banshee* is young men (16-26). The exploitation and abuse of women is very bad for this age group for a variety of reasons.

According to ChatGPT Bard (2023), *"The depiction of brutal rape in movies, video games, and television shows can be harmful to young men between the ages of 16 and 26 for several reasons — creating a number of negative consequences for young people.*

*First, young men are at a critical stage of brain development during this time. The prefrontal cortex, which is responsible for decision-making and impulse control, is still developing. This means that young men may be more susceptible to the effects of violent media.*

*Second, watching rape can normalize violence against women. When young men are exposed to media that depicts violence against women, it can normalize this behavior in their minds. This can make them more likely to engage in violent or abusive behavior towards women in their own lives.*

*Third, it can desensitize young men to violence against women. When young men are constantly exposed to violence against women, they can become desensitized to it. This can make them less likely to speak out against violence against women, or to intervene when they see it happening.*

*Fourth, young men are more likely to engage in risky behaviors, such as substance abuse and violence. This is due in part to the fact that their brains are still developing, and they are more likely to act impulsively.*

*Fifth, it can be harmful to the mental health of young men. Exposure to violence against women can be traumatic for young men and can lead to post-traumatic stress disorder (PTSD) and other mental health problems.*

*Sixth, young men are more likely to be exposed to violent media than other age groups. This is because they are more likely to play video games, watch movies, and television shows that are rated for mature audiences.*

*In addition to these specific concerns, there is also a consensus that media violence can have a negative impact on children and adolescents. The American Academy of Pediatrics (AAP) has issued a policy statement on media violence that states: "Media violence can increase the risk of aggressive behavior, especially in boys and adolescents who are already at risk for such behavior."*

*The AAP also notes that "media violence can also increase children's fear and anxiety and can desensitize them to violence."*

In other words, by creating these violent shows, the CIA Checchi family cult leaders are programing young men for various kinds of violence. This is bad for society, bad for young men and bad for the families & communities in which they live.

Season 4, Episode 5 (35:00 minutes) shows a scene in a BDSM bar that mixes violence, pain and sex. According to ChatGPT (2023), *"BDSM (Bondage & Discipline, Dominance & Submission, Sadism & Masochism), involves consensual activities focused on power dynamics, sensation play, and various forms of physical and psychological stimulation. Individuals who engage in BDSM might identify with different roles such as Dominants, Submissives, Switches, etc.*

*It's important to note that engaging in BDSM activities requires informed consent, communication, and a thorough understanding of boundaries between all involved parties. This practice isn't inherently pathological or indicative of mental health issues; instead, it's about exploring different aspects of sexuality and personal preferences within a safe and consensual framework.*

*There's no single explanation for why individuals are drawn to BDSM. For some, it might be about exploring power dynamics, experiencing intense sensations, or finding emotional release through controlled pain. It can also be a way to express intimacy, trust, and vulnerability with a partner.*

*Whether society should encourage or discourage such lifestyles is a complex ethical and moral question. Advocates argue that as long as activities are consensual and safe, individuals have the right to explore their sexual preferences without judgment or stigma. Others might argue that mainstream encouragement could normalize behavior that might not align with societal values or might not be appropriate for everyone.*

*In a society that openly acknowledges and supports alternative lifestyles like BDSM, there might be increased acceptance and understanding of diverse sexual preferences. However, the degree to which a society encourages or discourages any specific lifestyle can vary greatly based on cultural, ethical, and moral norms prevailing in that society.*

*Encouraging diversity and respect for individual choices while ensuring education about consent and safety could contribute to a society that values personal autonomy and sexual freedom. However, without proper education and understanding, there might be misunderstandings or misconceptions that could lead to societal stigmatization or even unsafe practices.*

*Ultimately, it's crucial to approach discussions about alternative lifestyles like BDSM with an emphasis on informed consent, communication, and mutual respect, recognizing that people have diverse sexual preferences and practices."*

It's important to point out that the CIA Checchi family cult kills people based on their involvement in such practices. They see this BDSM culture as perverted, depraved, and unhealthy for society. The Checchi's encourage this through their spies in the gay community and in shows like this only to draw out people who have this kind of interest, so they can be killed. When killing gay people and people into BDSM, they have made billions of dollars for themselves. Highlighting BDSM in a show like this gives them bait with which to lure people into this lifestyle.

I know this is true because during my court case against them, they tried (for over three years) to falsely tie me to the BDSM, kink and fetish community – which gives them justification to kill freaky, perverse, aberrant people. As ChatGPT (2023) says, *"This [BDSM] practice isn't inherently pathological or indicative of mental health issues."* But don't tell that to the conservative Supreme Court Justices who decide these issues in secret proceedings held for the CIA Checchi family cult leaders. The CIA Checchi cult leaders know they can sway the conservative Court Justices to be on their side on this issue – therefore, making a mockery of the Honorable Court. Falsely accused "deviant" people are incorrectly found guilty and condemn to death or in the least, condemned to be slaves of the CIA Checchi family cult.

### DRUGS (ADULT CONTENT) (AC)

The CIA Checchi cult leaders are the biggest drug dealers on Earth. From the poppy fields in Afghanistan to the cocaine cartels in Columbia, the CIA Checchi cult leaders control it all – again, reaping billions worldwide in drug trafficking. Drugs also brings them into the world of guns, which they are also trafficking worldwide.

Season 1, episode 2 (31:25) *"These raves are highly organized enterprises, designed for the sole purpose of selling drugs. Where there are drugs, there will be guns."*

Season 1, episode 2, (42:09) they tie in a Senator in Washington, D.C. with one of the student drug-deaths at the rave. What they reveal in this scene is that they routinely bully political leaders into doing what they are told to do by threatening or attacking their children, grandchildren, or other family members. Political leaders hold tremendous power in a democracy. So, a show about the CIA Checchi criminal empire would not be complete without politicians appearing as significant people whom they use for their own greedy purposes, personal financial prosperity, and to solidify their power base.

In real life, bullying, threatening, attacking, and abusing the relatives of political leaders is Standard Operating Procedure for the CIA Checchi family. More needs to be done to protect public servants from the terrorism, bribery, bullying, and abuse which the CIA Checchi family brings into the lives of political, military, and judicial leaders.

On September 13, 2023 the CIA Checchi family cult leaders launched a new attack on the rule of law by killing the husband of a lawmaker in Congress and they tried to frame President Biden for the murder because he is not cooperating 100% with their plan to destroy American democracy (they tried to suggest that Biden was unhappy with the conversation he had with Congresswoman Peltola on Air Force One on 9/11, which has been widely covered by the media: *"After the [9/11] commemoration [in Alaska], Representative Peltola traveled to Washington, D.C. on Air Force [One] with President Biden. On the flight, they were expected to discuss the President's trip to Asia and Alaska's role in Pacific Rim strategy and energy markets."*

https://www.yahoo.com/news/rep-mary-peltolas-husband-died-145904996.html).

The murder of this lawmaker's husband is another example of how the CIA Checchi family cult leaders are trying to undermine American democracy, intimidate political leaders and destroy the rule of law in America. This CIA family has been killing people who uphold the rule of law and also killing family members of those who uphold the rule of law. Representative Peltola is the kind of dedicated legislator that would stand up to the corrupt CIA Checchi family. The list of politicians, judges, attorneys and law enforcement people the Checchi's have killed over the last twenty years is very long.

Another example in *Banshee* regarding the connection to powerful political leaders can be seen in season 4, episode 8 (the last episode of the series – 2:19 minutes) they reveal the connections between the dark criminal world of the Aryan Brotherhood and a powerful politician who pulls the strings behind it all. Translation: there are compromised politicians who are not working for the American people, but instead, they work for the dark Checchi terrorist cartel that controls groups like the Aryan Brotherhood.

## ADULT SEX SCENES (NUDITY) (N)

There are many, many scenes in *Banshee* that are filmed inside a strip bar which ensures to hold the attention of a 16-26 male audience of college students, military recruits, and others. The number of explicit sex scenes are so numerous it would take too much space to list them all here (nearly every single episode features constant, explicit sex scenes).

## CHILD INTIMACY SCENES

The Checchi's play a dangerous and lucrative game with *Banshee*. They show a tremendous amount of teenage skin, teenage scenes depicting intimacy and sex. Some of these scenes are technically "legal" but there is an unspoken rule about government agents being allowed to frame people with "teenagers" who are legally adults (18, 19 years old). In this show, they continually trick people into watching the sexualization of teens of every age.

For example, at a rave held in the barn of a vacationing Amish person. In season 1, episode 9 (5:30) we see the uncle lusting after his 19-year-old niece who has left the Amish farm to come and live with him and help him run his various businesses (a strip club, a slaughterhouse, an ecstasy/drug manufacturing facility, etc.).

Season 1, episode 2 (11 minutes) features a male adult casually attempting to have sex with a female high school student (15 years old).

Season 1, episode 2 (32 minutes) – high school students at a rave doing drugs, being sexual. Anyone watching this can be put on a watch list for potentially being interested in underage sex. It's a trap, wrapped in a TV show and serves to create an atmosphere of undue influence, encouraging sex with teens as something that "everyone does."

Season 2 Episode 3 – children being intimate. Aimed at influencing children who might be watching and aimed at adults who might like to watch children in situations like this. This is another CIA Checchi family trap.

Season 3 Episode 6 – The Checchi's promote their teenage "family" cult. At 31:45 viewers see inside a house full of young people/students doing drugs, drinking, being sexually intimate, playing video games. One teen says to the other, *"you people live here together? We're just like any other family except we actually take care of each other."* Manipulatively capitalizing on a young viewer's desire to belong to a group, a "family" if their own biological family does not understand them (which is a very typical feeling and experience that many teenagers have regarding their biological family at some point during teenage years.). This scene is a PR stunt to promote the Checchi's own cult ("family") in which millions of teens worldwide are part.

## TRAINING COPS HOW TO BE BAD COPS

The level of police deception, lies, and fraud in *Banshee* is astronomical. In season 1, episode 4 (23:06) you see one of many illegal police actions, *"Hey cop. What the fuck are you doing here* [no warrant, just walks in]*? (Cop throws questioning citizen into the wall, head first) "Whatever the fuck I want."* The CIA Checchi family cult has thousands of police and law enforcement professionals throughout the country that are members of the Checchi cult. They raise their spies into positions of power by setting up crimes in which their police become involved in busting. After numerous situations in which these spy-police are involved, they get promoted higher and higher up the chain of command. Manipulative ploys is how they get their spies into positions of power within various police organizations – from state police, sheriffs and local police chiefs in small and large towns throughout America. They even train some of their spies on how to beat a lie detector test (which is required for many police jobs). The easiest way to beat a lie detector test is to make sure it's one of your spies giving the test – ensuring easy questions, which makes passing this test easy. Once they have their spies in charge of the police, there is not a crime they can't get away with in that jurisdiction. This is how they get away with prolific drug crimes, killing people, and much more. They create a system into which witnesses, evidence of crimes, and genuine justice disappear into a black hole.

## TRAINING THIEVES ON HOW TO ROB BUSINESSES

For over fifty years in America, this has been the rule: If the CIA Checchi family cult leaders 'don't own the business, they run it. If they don't run the business, they burn it down' (which is made clear in season 1, episode 1 of *Banshee*).

It's important to control all businesses because this gives the CIA Checchi family cult control of all money going to individual people. Control the money and you control the people. Control the people, you control the families. Control the families, you control the community. Control the community, you control the local county. Control the counties, you control the state. Control the states, you control the country.

Season 3, episode 1 (25:15), Police officer to high school student caught stealing from a business after hours: *"So, you want to be a thief now? A little piece of advice… it's harder than you think. Your first mistake was your numbers. Every extra person increases your chances of getting caught, and you have three people in a one-man job. Not a great start. Come with me. See an alarm on the door? Window? No. So how did I get here so fast? See that little white box up there? It's a sound sensor. You break the glass that triggers the silent alarm 10 seconds later my office is on the radio. Here I am. Your only option with glasses and cutter. So, this is it, huh? Jackpot. How much did you get?*

*Student: $37.*

*Police Officer: Wow. The register is also connected to the alarm, so you would have been better to take the whole thing and open it when you got clear, although. If there is any real cash left overnight. It's going to be in the safe (shows student where safe is hidden), which is also bolted to the floor. So, you know how to crack a safe?*

*Student: Nope.*

*Police Officer: Well then, there's really nothing in here worth getting arrested for. Unless, of course, that was the point.*

*Student: You think I wanted to get caught?*

*Police: Self destruction runs in the family."*

## WHITE SUPREMACY

It seems that *Banshee* is also used to encourage and communicate with white supremacists. In this show the Aryan Brotherhood (*"a neo-Nazi prison gang and an organized crime syndicate which is based in the United States and has an estimated 15,000–20,000 members both inside and outside prisons."* https://en.wikipedia.org/wiki/Aryan_Brotherhood) is depicted in a positive, righteous light.

According to ChatGPT Bard (2023), *"White supremacists are a group of people who believe that white people are superior to other races. They often hold racist, anti-Semitic, and homophobic beliefs. White supremacists have been responsible for numerous acts of violence and terrorism, including the Oklahoma City bombing and the Charlottesville, Virginia rally that resulted in the death of one person.*

*The core beliefs of white supremacy vary depending on the specific group, but they generally include the following:*

*The belief that white people are a superior race.*

*The belief that white people are being persecuted by other races.*

*The belief that white people need to protect their culture and way of life.*

*White supremacists often use violence and intimidation to try to achieve their goals. They have been known to target minority groups with violence, harassment, and threats. They have also been known to infiltrate law enforcement and the military in an attempt to gain access to weapons and training.*

*White supremacy is a dangerous and harmful ideology that has no place in our society. It is important to be aware of the dangers of white supremacy and to speak out against it whenever possible."*

The CIA Checchi family has made sure they control and protect white supremacists for their own purposes. For example, the Checchi's have turned the American prison system into a racial hierarchy and placed the white supremacy group at the top of the pyramid (and black people at the bottom). I write more about what the CIA Checchi family has done to the jail & prison system in America in my book *"Six Months in L.A. County Jail"* at this link: https://1drv.ms/b/s!AszYNXg2gQYImUYJX1ERJB-0vOqF?e=JQz3nF (a paperback book is also available for purchase at Amazon.com https://www.amazon.com/Eight-Months-County-Jail-Dysfunctional/dp/1731408528). The CIA Checchi family have turned the prison system in the United States into a massive racial battleground and much more.

The Checchi's use the Aryan Brotherhood as their main front for drug trafficking, arms (gun) trafficking, murder, and general chaos creators. *"According to the Federal Bureau of Investigation (FBI), the Aryan Brotherhood was founded in California and controls the West Coast and Southwestern U.S. throughout the federal prison system. There activities include murder, assault, drug trafficking, robbery, gambling, extortion, racketeering, arms trafficking, inmate prostitution, human trafficking, dog fighting. The Aryan Brotherhood makes up an extremely low percentage of the entire US prison population, but it is responsible for a disproportionately large number of prison murders. By the 1990s, the Aryan Brotherhood had shifted its focus away from killing for strictly racial reasons and focused on organized crime such as drug trafficking, prostitution, and sanctioned murders."* https://en.wikipedia.org/wiki/Aryan_Brotherhood

The CIA Checchi cult leaders go out of their way to protect people from this criminal gang, saving them from the harshest penalties. They can manipulate the system because the Checchi's control so many judges, attorneys, parole boards, etc. As a bonus the Checchi's also provide incarcerated gang members with drugs while inside a prison because these gang members are an important part of the Checchi's corrupt criminal empire. Here's one example of what they do for these notorious gang members: *"In late 2002, 29 leaders of the [Aryan Brotherhood] gang were simultaneously rounded up from prisons all over the country and brought to trial under the Racketeer Influenced and Corrupt Organizations (RICO) Act. The intention was to bring death sentences for at least 21 of them, in a manner similar to tactics used against organized crime. The case produced 30 convictions but none of the most powerful leaders received a death sentence. Sentencing occurred in March 2006 for three of the most powerful leaders of the gang, including Barry Mills and Tyler Bingham, who were indicted for numerous crimes, including murder, conspiracy, drug trafficking, and racketeering and for ordering killings and beatings from their cells. Bingham and Mills were convicted of murder and sent back to United States Penitentiary Administrative Maximum Facility Prison (ADX) in Florence, Colorado, escaping the death penalty."* https://en.wikipedia.org/wiki/Aryan_Brotherhood

In the last two seasons of *Banshee*, the Checchi's make sure to give White Supremacy some airtime and tell their story as seekers of justice in a corrupt country that has lost its way. For example, Season 4 episode 2, the Aryan Brotherhood leader tells his friend the CIA Checchi family motto, *"Fortune favors the bold. Power comes from doing whatever it takes. Justice at any cost…"* These are words put into the production to help inspire and encourage lawless behavior of White Supremacy groups. This program is also a training tool for white supremacy groups.

While this is going on, it is interspaced with a religious service of Amish people singing the old Christian hymn that has the words, "God in three persons, blessed Trinity…" This is significant because it refers to the three Checchi knuckleheads who run a large part of the Checchi cult: David Kanuth, Adam Checchi and Michael Fisher. These CIA Checchi cult leaders are genuine in their belief that they are divine. They are preoccupied with their own divinity. (I wish I was joking about this, but it's real. There's nothing like watching a group of obviously flawed and broken people seriously believing they are Devine Gods). They believe they are God in three persons, the blessed Trinity. When I first heard this nonsense from them, I thought they were joking. It is not a joke. They believe they are God. Last I checked with a psychologist, this sort of belief has something to do with mental illness.

Every episode of *Banshee* has multiple butt shots centered in the screen. Centering things in the center of the computer or TV screen makes it more likely that people will focus on it. It is deliberate manipulation for people to view, and be judged on (failing the "eye test") and reaping millions of dollars for the CIA Checchi family cult.

## THE KNICK

There are too many shows on Apple+ to review in this way. Every show I've seen has scenes that the CIA Checchi family cult has manipulated so that they can frame people for looking at butts and breasts. Even with shows and scenes that seem harmless, the cult leaders have coordinated things so that people can be framed and accused of inappropriate or perverted behavior. In the show *The Knick* season 1, episode 3 (33:00 minutes) the creators have situated a pig butt in the direct line of sight of the main speaker, a woman. For 30 seconds the viewer is forced to view the pig butt as they watch the woman speak. Yes, even animal butts are a violation of the rules in this bizzarro CIA Checchi family "eye testing" program. Viewers are not allowed to look at any butts – people or animals.

# 3 BUTTS AND BREASTS
# ENTRAPMENT AND UNDUE INFLUENCE

According to ChatGPT (2023), *"Entrapment and undue influence are legal concepts that play significant roles in the American legal system, particularly in criminal and contract law.*

## *Entrapment:*

*Entrapment occurs when law enforcement officials* [or government agents] *induce or persuade an individual to commit a crime that they were not predisposed to commit. It involves coercing or luring someone who is naïve and gullible into committing an offense that they otherwise wouldn't have committed without the persuasion, influence or pressure from a spy, government agent or law enforcement person.*

*Importance in the legal system:*

*Entrapment is crucial because it protects individuals from unfair or improper tactics used by government agents or law enforcement agencies to incite criminal behavior. It upholds the principles of justice by ensuring that individuals are not unfairly targeted or induced into doing things or committing crimes they wouldn't have otherwise engaged in. Courts examine whether the individual had a predisposition to commit the crime or if an agent of the government's actions led to the commission of the offense.*

**Undue Influence:**

*Undue influence refers to the exertion of improper pressure or persuasion on someone to enter into a contract or make decisions against their best interests. It involves one party taking advantage of a position of power, trust, or authority to manipulate another party into making a decision they wouldn't have otherwise made.*

*Importance in the legal system:*

*In contract law, undue influence is crucial because it protects individuals from being coerced or manipulated into agreements that they would not have entered into voluntarily. It ensures that contracts are entered into freely, without any party taking advantage of the other's vulnerability or using unfair tactics to secure an agreement. Courts examine the nature of the relationship between the parties and whether there was an imbalance of power or if the vulnerable party was exploited.*

*Both concepts are essential because they safeguard individual rights and prevent abuses of power. They serve to maintain the fairness and integrity of the legal system by ensuring that individuals are not unjustly coerced, manipulated, or entrapped into actions or agreements that they wouldn't have pursued under normal circumstances."*

It's common for things on my computer to just randomly pop up on my computer screen, like this screen shot copied here:

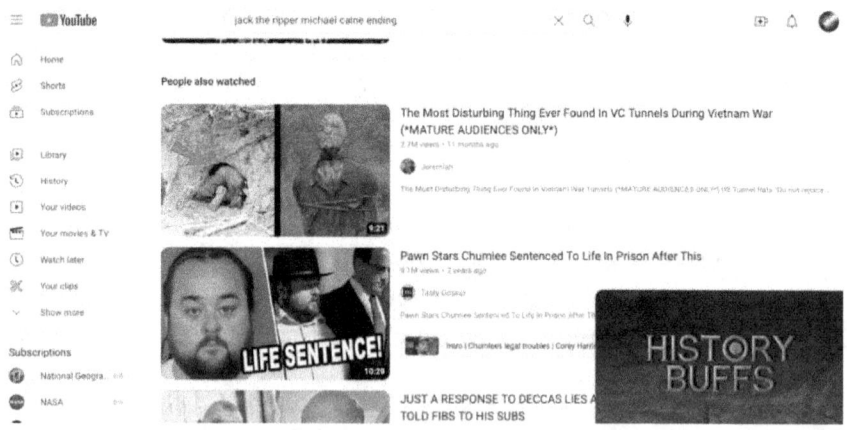

Notice the guy's butt sticking out of a cave, with the red arrow pointing at it. This kind of nonsense goes on daily on my computer as they attempt to frame me as a creep obsessed with butts. If you look at the red arrow in the screen shot (which is pointing at the guy's butt as he enters a cave) you will see an example of the CIA Checchi family's psychological manipulation. The CIA has been doing experiments on mind control and manipulation for as long as the CIA has existed. The Checchi's get paid for making people look at where the arrow is pointing. If you look at his butt for more than two seconds, it qualifies you to "flunk" their eye test. If you look at his butt, the CIA Checchi family terrorists use this "data" as proof that you are a sick person sexualizing someone's butt. This sort of "eye testing" is complete nonsense. I have hundreds and hundreds of examples like this of things they have done to me on my computer.

You'll also see evidence in this screen shot of the CIA Checchi family threatening me with a "life sentence" for exposing their criminal empire. They are trying to have me arrested and put in jail for the rest of my life because I exposed their prolific murders of genocide and their high-volume abuse of children.

When I am online anywhere – whether I'm looking at Twitter, email, videos on YouTube, State Police notices, Yahoo news or advertising – I have been trained for many, many years to look at all the details of a photo or the written text of a message in order to understand the hidden message being sent via the photo or text. It is common for spies and spy agencies to secretly communicate through these public avenues. Photos and written words (the text) often hold coded information, hidden in plain sight.

Why do they communicate this way? Because this is how clandestine people communicate. Spy agencies and spy masters like the CIA Checchi family terrorist cult leaders don't normally send emails or letters explaining directly what they want someone to know or what they want someone to do. They must be sneakier than that.

More often than not, hidden within the details of a picture or in the text of a news report or an email, there is information that must be decoded. I personally think this is incredibly inefficient because there is too much room for miscommunication, double messages, and just sloppy craftsmanship. I've come to despise this indirect method of communication because it is prone to misinterpretation, sometimes remains hidden or in the case of sexually provocative content, is often used to trap someone as some sort of "proof" that they are sick. The Checchi's are very experienced at trapping people with this sort of manipulated nonsense.

Any reasonable person would agree that it is 100% unethical to train someone to look at all the details of a photo or news article at a website and then condemn him/her for looking at all the details of a photo or news article when they are trying to trap him/her and frame him/her as a predator or creep.

For example, the Checchi's often start putting up photos of kids on my various social media feeds. Apparently, I'm not supposed to look at those photos for more than two seconds because if I do, it is proof that I am some kind of child predator. Once you get someone in the habit of studying all the details of their external environment or the details of a photo or news article online, it's garbage science and garbage "data" to then claim that person is a creepy predator for doing what they have been trained to do.

Because this CIA Checchi family nonsense has been going on for over three decades in my life, it has become routine and habitual to analyze and look closely at everything – from my external environment to photos and news articles online. I've been doing it for so many years, it's beyond habit – performed without conscious thought.

The Checchi's attempt to try to frame anyone as a creep because they now use these pathways of online communication to make someone look at a variety of pictures meant to trap that person, is beyond ridiculous. It's complete Checchi nonsense and garbage science. It's more about Checchi entrapment and undue influence than it is science. I've been complaining to authorities at the CIA and the military about this Checchi abuse for a very long time (see letter below to CIA Director).

A psychologist could explain this better than I can... but if you inundate someone with the same pictures (for example, a picture of nothing but shorts with a bulge at the zipper or a close up photo of a woman with large breasts wearing a tight t-shirt) and you tell someone "don't look at the crotch" or "don't look at the large breasts"... there is some kind of psychological trick that makes someone who never looked at these things to all of the sudden look at them. The same is true with the pink elephant example (as you read this, don't think about a pink elephant or any elephant).

If you show these same pictures of breasts or crotch shots over and over (as the Checchi's do to thousands of people online, for example) there is something about this Checchi-scam that makes it a psychological trick. You can trick someone into looking at things, that they normally would not look at by repetitively making these photos appear on their computer.

If I told you not to yawn right now. DO NOT THINK OF YAWNING. Don't yawn. You might be finding yourself suppressing a yawn or you might yawn. Yawning is a sign that you are guilty and anxious – so don't yawn. Don't do it. These kinds of suggestions are the type of psychological tricks that people who are professional manipulators practice every day.

As ChatGPT explains, *"The phenomenon you're referring to is often described as "thought suppression" or the "ironic process theory." It's the concept where actively trying to suppress or avoid certain thoughts makes those thoughts more persistent or likely to surface in the mind.*

*Instructing someone not to think about a pink elephant while reading immediately draws attention to the idea of a pink elephant. This directive tends to have the opposite effect, causing the individual's mind to focus more on the specific thing they were told not to think about.*

*This phenomenon has been widely studied and is a part of cognitive psychology, illustrating how the human mind processes information and handles attempts to control or suppress thoughts.*

*This technique is often used as a psychological manipulation or a persuasive tool by certain individuals to influence or control others' behaviors, thoughts, or reactions. By drawing attention to something and emphasizing the prohibition or avoidance of it, it can paradoxically heighten one's focus or inclination toward that specific action or thought.*

*The technique you're describing, repeatedly showing certain images or content to desensitize or provoke a reaction, is known as 'exposure therapy' or 'exposure conditioning.' However, the context you provided, involving repetitive and explicit imagery in a deliberate attempt to attract attention or manipulate people's reactions, might be more aligned with a tactic referred to as 'shock advertising' or 'shock marketing.'*

*Shock advertising involves using provocative or controversial images, often considered taboo or forbidden, to elicit a strong emotional response, grab attention, or create buzz around a product, service, or message. This technique aims to break through the clutter of traditional advertising by relying on the shock value of the content to engage the audience and leave a lasting impression.*

*In the specific context you mentioned, where repetitive display of certain images—like bra commercials or provocative attire—is used to provoke curiosity or attract attention, it might be considered a form of shock advertising or exposure to desensitize and normalize taboo or forbidden imagery."*

Here is one example from April 14, 2023, where they constantly put up a picture of a teenager on my computer. If I'm not mistaken, it's a picture of him when he joined the military as a teenager, but when writing about him in the headline, they claim he is 21 years old.

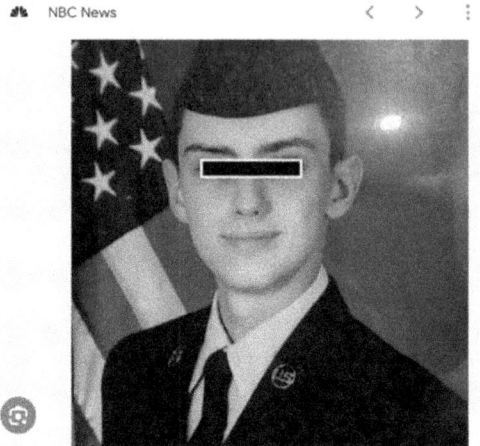

NBC News

FBI arrests 21-year-old Air National Guardsman suspected of leaking classified documents

Visit >

The recent (2023) pictures of this young military man shown by other news outlets on the same day didn't have him looking this young (he broke the law by sharing classified information. No doubt he is a Checchi spy, and he was following orders to do what he did). This age game with teen photos is more Checchi nonsense which they do to thousands of people online in an effort to get people to look at Checchi-manipulated content. This is more Checchi garbage science, more Checchi entrapment and undue influence.

This issue is very concerning beyond my own experience. It is an issue for all Americans to be concerned about because they are playing these manipulative games with thousands and thousands of people. They are putting innocent, gullible people in grave danger and the Checchi's are making millions and millions of dollars (billions of dollars over decades) from this manipulative junk science as they trick people into looking at things on the internet... and use this as proof that they are finding perverted, creepy people who are threats to their community – threats to national security.

When you realize that there is a massive push to bring broadband (Killer Broadband) into every community, now you know why: they want to make billions of dollars more by finding more victims they can manipulate and fool with their sophisticated CIA psychology tricks.

In a small number of cases, they might be finding people who are genuine threats to the community, threats to national security. But this would be true with any sample of the population. The recent big push by the Biden-Harris administration to get broadband high-speed internet into all rural communities in America is, in reality, being pushed by the CIA Checchi family terrorists from the shadows where they lurk. They want to make more money from using this junk "eye testing" crap… to trap, trick and manipulate more innocent, naïve Americans into their web of entrapment and undue influence by growing this program of "eye testing" and "eye trickery" on the internet. This is more CIA Checchi family abuse of power and another way the Checchi terrorists can deceive citizens into their webs of unethical manipulation.

As with all Checchi spy games and situations of undue influence & entrapment, even if someone would have done something illegal, there is no chance they would be guilty of any crime during this time because, as it says on the Department of Justice website on entrapment, "Government agents may not originate a criminal design, implant in an innocent person's mind the disposition to commit a criminal act, and then induce commission of the crime so that the Government may prosecute." Jacobson v. United States, 503 U.S. 540, 548 (1992); Sorrells v. United States, 287 U. S. 435, 442; Mathews v. United States, 485 U.S. 58, 63 (1988).

According to ChatGPT (2023), "*These legal cases—Jacobson v. United States, Sorrells v. United States, and Mathews v. United States—deal with the concept of entrapment in criminal law in the context of undue influence and government conduct.*

***Sorrells v. United States (1932)****: In this case, the U.S. Supreme Court discussed entrapment. It established that when the government induces someone to commit a crime they were not predisposed to commit, it constitutes entrapment. This ruling emphasizes the importance of the defendant's predisposition to commit the crime and whether the government's actions led to inducing an otherwise unwilling person to commit the offense.*

KILLER BROADBAND

*Jacobson v. United States (1992)*: *This case reasserted the principles laid out in Sorrells v. United States. It clarified that the government's actions could be seen as entrapment if they induced an individual to commit a crime they were not predisposed to commit.*

*Mathews v. United States (1988)*: *This case, along with the others, revolves around entrapment principles. It emphasized the importance of examining the defendant's predisposition to commit the crime when determining if entrapment occurred.*

*In the context of entrapment and undue influence, these cases help establish legal standards and considerations for determining whether a person was coerced or induced by governmental actions to commit a crime they would not have otherwise committed.*

*Entrapment occurs when law enforcement officials* [spies, or government agents] *use tactics that induce an individual to do something they were not predisposed to do. Undue influence, on the other hand, involves various forms of pressure or persuasion* [tricks of manipulation] *that significantly affect an individual's decision-making, potentially leading them to engage in actions they might not have otherwise taken. While these legal cases primarily focus on entrapment, they contribute to the broader understanding of how government conduct and undue influence can impact criminal cases."*

"Undue influence" is excessive persuasion that causes a person to act or refrain from acting in a certain way, and it has resulted in constant unfairness, tremendous injustice & inequity. It is a fact that because the CIA Checchi family targets thousands of people with their manipulative games, these innocent people are genuine victims of extreme, calculated undue influence.

The definition of undue influence in California state law is in California Civil Code § 1575 which was enacted in 1872. *"The elements of that definition which are still in effect for contract law are: 1) The use, by one in whom a confidence is reposed by another, or who holds real or apparent authority over him, of such confidence or authority for the purpose of obtaining an unfair advantage over him; 2) In taking unfair advantage of another's weakness of mind; and 3) In taking a grossly oppressive and unfair advantage of another' necessities or distress* (https://www.americanbar.org/groups/law_aging/publications/bifo cal/vol_35/issue_3_feb2014/defining_undue_influence/).

CIA Checchi family tricks include killing innocent people and then going after loved ones of the deceased person while they are in a vulnerable emotional state of grieving. When they kill someone, they create a massive emotional hole in the lives of the loved ones left behind as they grieve.

The Checchi's can also keep surviving loved ones very isolated during this time of grief. Sometimes depriving these people of genuine affection and genuine friendships. (In my own life, it was during this time after they killed my parents that they surrounded me exclusively with Checchi spies who attempted to manipulate drugs and drug culture into my life. Due to my conservative Christian roots, drugs were something I had been against all my life. These drugs were meant to eventually kill me. But I was able to avoid this final, fatal Checchi trap of death.)

*"New research study prompted the second response: landmark legislation modernizing the definition of undue influence. The new definition took effect January 1, 2014, and affects probate matters such as conservatorships, wills, and trusts. The new definition was also placed in the state's Welfare and Institutions Code, addressing the financial abuse of an elder or a dependent adult.*

*The language is the same in both codes and consists of the following: "Undue influence" means excessive persuasion that causes another person to act or refrain from acting by overcoming that person's free will and results in inequity. In determining whether a result was produced by undue influence, all of the following shall be considered: 1) Vulnerability of the victim. Evidence of vulnerability may include, but is not limited to, incapacity, illness disability, injury, age, education, impaired cognitive function, emotional distress, isolation, or dependency where the influencer knew of, or should have known of, the alleged victim's vulnerability. 2) The influencer's apparent authority. Evidence of apparent authority may include but is not limited to, status as a fiduciary, family member, care provider, health care processional, legal professional, spiritual adviser, expert, or other qualification. 3) The actions or tactics used by the influencer. Evidence of actions or tactics used may include, but is not limited to, all of the following: a) Controlling necessaries of life, medication, the victim's interactions with others, access to information or sleep. b) Use of affection, intimidation, or coercion. c) Initiation of changes in person or property rights, use of haste or secrecy in effecting those changes, effecting changes at inappropriate time and places, and claims of expertise in effecting change. 4) The equity of the result. Evidence of the equity of the result may include, but is not limited to, the economic consequences to the victim, any divergence from the victim's prior intent or course of conduct or dealing, the relationship of the value conveyed to the value of any services or consideration received, or the appropriateness of the change in light of the length and nature of*

*the relationship. Evidence of an inequitable result, without more, is not sufficient to prove undue influence."* This information was obtained from the American Bar Association:
https://www.americanbar.org/groups/law_aging/publications/bifoc al/vol_35/issue_3_feb2014/defining_undue_influence/

As Dr. Harry E. Morgan says, becoming susceptible to undue influence *"can happen to people with a clear capacity if there are sufficient strategic efforts to change their beliefs and provide them with the fallacious information… Even someone with full cognitive capacity can be made vulnerable and weakened."* (https://www.youtube.com/watch?v=d6DJEIXu-VE&list=TLPQMjkwNzIwMjI00B66EtWElQ&index=4)

For over fifty years, the CIA has trained people on how to control people's minds and even brainwash people through tactics of psychological manipulation and undue influence. The CIA Checchi family has used these tested and scientifically based tools to manipulate the lives of thousands and thousands of innocent, naïve American citizens.

A social psychologist, Dr. Dina McMillan, said in her lecture (video link to the lecture is below): *"In social psychology, we study influence and interaction. We look at the factors that can change beliefs and behaviors - often without someone consciously noticing. So, we examine methods of persuasion, manipulation, and coercion…. Your life can be ruined by someone who never puts his hands on you in anger. Coercive control is living under a suffocating system where someone else controls every aspect of your life. What you do, say, eat, how you dress, where and how you live, whether you get an education or have a job, how you spend your money, how many children you have and how you interact with them. Your relationships are monitored – even with your own family, and you can't have relationships at all unless the person controlling you gives their permission. With no exaggeration, it's a type of slavery…. They felt entitled to a relationship that is all in their favor, where they can be hyper-controlling and cruel, and the person just had to accept it…. These early tactics are known as 'grooming.' Grooming is scripted behavior with a purpose. It's saying and doing things to lure someone in, inspiring their trust, intensifying their emotional attachment, and increasing control. All these tactics belong to a group of influence techniques known as 'psychological manipulation.' Psychological manipulation is lying, deceiving, and performing in order to influence how someone thinks, feels and acts…. Psychological manipulation is scary because it's not only effective; it works whether you recognize it or not, agree to it or not, resist it or not. Your only protection, your only defense, is to get away from the person using them on you."*

(Dr. McMillan's talk is here at this link:
https://www.youtube.com/watch?v=ythOTBEkUZM).

Without my knowledge or consent, I had been slowly spellbound and gradually caught in a massive CIA Checchi family web of deliberate deception, careful manipulation, and thoughtful duplicity.

HOW TO CREATE A WEB OF UNDUE INFLUENCE

The first rule of creating a web of undue influence is to be subtle, understated, elusive. This wisdom comes from the oldest military play book on Earth: *The Art of War* by Master S. Tzu (written around the 5th century BCE – 2,500 years ago):

## *"Be extremely subtle, even to the point of formlessness. Be extremely mysterious, even to the point of soundlessness. Thereby you can be the director of the opponent's fate."*

A quote from *The Art of War*, by Master S. Tzu

The CIA Checchi family's empire -which is built on games of undue influence and entrapment- is massive. The tools and methods they employ to manipulate people and influence behavior are usually very subtle. If subtle games and understated tools are used constantly and in various ways, you can be the 'director of the opponent's fate.'

The Checchi family frequently leverages already established celebrities across various artistic fields. Music, in particular, wields significant influence in today's world. In typical business scenarios, celebrities are not immune to complying with the demands of the CIA Checchi family cult leaders. Should musicians, actors, or other artists follow the Checchi family's directives, they stand to gain financial benefits, promotions, coveted awards, and more. Conversely, failure to adhere to these instructions can result in the termination of their careers or even endanger their lives.

This trend has persisted for many decades, affecting artists ranging from Madonna (who thrives) to Michael Jackson (who was killed). The rules, rewards, and punishments enforced by the CIA Checchi family remain consistent across all artistic fields, distorting the essence of what it means to be an artist. When an artist is deprived of the freedom to live an authentic, sincere, and honest life, they lose connection with the wellspring of Creativity, which some people call God. The only language God speaks is the language of sincerity, which is connected to integrity and authenticity. Working as a tool for the forces of manipulation, deceit, and duplicity (which the CIA Checchi family represents and leads) may yield financial gain, but it severs the artist from the ultimate sources of fulfillment in life: sincerity and love, which cultivates profound joy and inner peace. One cannot divorce love and kindness from sincerity, integrity, and creativity.

An entire book could be written about hundreds of artists and their work as conduits of undue influence - as it relates to the CIA Checchi family empire. In this book, I'll just point out two examples from the artists Christina Aguilera and Willie Nelson. Christina has a song she performs with Maroon 5 that was released in 2011, called *Moves Like Jagger*. To watch a video of Christina performing part of *Moves Like Jagger*, click here:
https://www.youtube.com/watch?v=8UT9ZAtHgGw&list=WL&index=69

The Song *Moves Like Jagger* can be interpreted in various ways. On one level it seems to be a song about a young female stripper / prostitute who sells sex to older men. This is a crime which the song celebrates and encourages. This song was raised to international fame and became part of the CIA Checchi family's undue influence machine. The song is useful for the CIA Checchi family cult because if they can get men and women to commit this crime, they can make money when they kill these people for being a bad influence in the community. To aid in getting people to commit this crime, a song like this can be helpful as a subtle form of CIA brainwashing, mind control and behavior influence.

## Lyrics: *Moves Like Jagger*

Just shoot for the stars, feels right
Aim for the heart, feel like
And take me away
And make it okay
I swear, I'll behave

You wanted control, we waited
I put on a show, now we're naked
You say, I'm a kid
My ego is big
I don't give a shit
And it goes like this

Take me by the tongue, and I'll know you
Kiss me till you're drunk, and I'll show you
All the moves like Jagger
I've got the moves like Jagger
I've got the moo-oo-oo-ooves like Jagger

I don't need to try to control you
Look into my eyes, and I'll own you
With the moves like Jagger
I've got the moves like Jagger
I've got the moo-oo-oo-ooves like Jagger

You wanna know how to make me smile
Take control, own me just for the night
And if I share my secret
You're gonna have to keep it
Nobody else can see this.

So watch and learn, I won't show you twice
Head to toe, ooh baby, rub me right yeah
If I share my secret
You're gonna have to keep it
Nobody else can see this (ay-yeah-yeah-yeah)

Take me by the tongue, and I'll know you
Kiss me till you're drunk, and I'll show you
All the moves like Jagger
I've got the moves like Jagger
I've got the moo-oo-oo-ooves like Jagger (woo)

I don't need to try to control you
Look into my eyes, and I'll own you
With the moves like Jagger
I've got the moves like Jagger
I've got the moo-oo-oo-ooves like Jagger

# *"This means being so subtle as to be imperceptible, and to be able to change suddenly like a mysterious spirit."*

A quote from *The Art of War*, by Master S. Tzu

Willie Nelson is an undisputed national treasure who has shared his music with millions of Americans for seven decades. Even Willie is forced to be part of the CIA Checchi family cult. Artists like Willy and Christina may or may not actually be aware of the ways that the CIA Checchi cult leaders use them for their machine of undue influence. The Checchi's are often able to use artists for their own financial gain when the artist has no idea exactly how they are being used.

An example of how the CIA Checchi family cult creates national situations of undue influence and entrapment in America can be seen in this one video celebrating Willie Nelson's 70th birthday. This is the kind of thing the CIA Checchi family uses to enslave countless people in America on the issue of marijuana. In 2023, marijuana is a Schedule One substance under the Controlled Substances Act - which at the time this was recorded, is the most serious felony. Getting celebrities who are under the control of the CIA Checchi cult (all of these celebrities in this video are either part of the CIA Checchi cult or targets of the CIA Checchi cult) to make fun of this drug and see them having a good time with it... creates a situation of undue influence and can even aid in creating a situation of entrapment for many Americans.

This video was recorded in New York City and is the kind of thing that one of the Checchi cult leaders would have conceived and had someone approach Willie and say, "it's your 70th birthday. Let's do a big TV special with lots of celebrities. It will make a lot of money." Hence, Willie Nelson & Friends "Live and Kicking" – 2003, was born.

Once the Checchi family gains control over politicians responsible for making laws, the police and judges who enforce those laws, and the celebrities who endorse lawbreaking activities, a powerful psychological influence emerges. This undue influence has the potential to impact millions, encouraging them to break laws. In this example, particularly the law prohibiting marijuana use.

As millions of American citizens disregard marijuana laws, the CIA Checchi family stands to profit immensely, generating billions of dollars from the illegal sale of marijuana in New York and across the country. Furthermore, they capitalize on enslaving those who violate the law under the pretext of Amendment 13 of the Constitution. *"Neither slavery nor involuntary servitude, **except as a punishment for crime** whereof the party shall have been duly convicted, shall exist within the United States, or any place subject to their jurisdiction."*

The CIA Checchi family can and does secretly enslave people into their cult based on criminal behavior. They can and do document these crimes with secret video and audio recordings. They can and do present these recordings in a secret court which the person in question may or may not be aware of. Because they are CIA people, they are cloaked with secrecy and the court proceedings are kept secret. I know this is true because they did this to me, and I spent almost four years in court fighting this CIA Checchi family nonsense. I discuss this legal slavery issue more in my book *"Reporting Child Abuse and CIA Abuse of Power."* You can also watch this 33-minute Public Service video about the CIA Checchi cult and their enslavement machine that makes slaves of people in America & throughout the world:
https://vimeo.com/848103183?share=copy

In this example video with Willie Nelson (link below), they got all their Checchi-spy celebrities to be part of this massive TV special in 2003. They were able to feature a song that promoted marijuana use. For decades the CIA Checchi family has used Willie to promote the illegal use of Marijuana. It is my theory that they forced Willie into cooperating with this scam starting in the early 1990s when Willie all the sudden had massive legal tax problems with the IRS. He had been manipulated to get involved in some business ventures that went awry. The Checchi's orchestrated these legal tax problems to help as a negotiation tactic to force Willie into their service on this issue. To watch the marijuana song, go to this link below and forward to 1:06:09 in the video timeline:

https://www.youtube.com/watch?v=a1veY6_nUcE&list=PLt_L-ABqnN-k_9i4ni2XxBADCImfkKw5g&index=262

Here below is a transcript of that part of the video and the song they sing.

Announcer: *Please welcome back Toby Keith.*

Toby Keith: *You all having a good time? Hey. All of these artists have one thing in common. We've all ended up on Willie's bus after the show, and me and my buddy Scott Emerick wrote a song about it. I think y'all can figure it out:*

I always heard that his herb was top shelf
Lord I just could not wait to find out for myself
Well don't knock it till you've tried it
And I've tried it my friend
I'll never smoke Weed with Willie again!

Now we learned a hard lesson in a small Texas town
He fired up a fat boy and he passed him around
The last words I spoke before they tucked me in
I may discount Bungee jump
But I'll never smoke weed with Willie again

I'll never smoke weed with Willie again
My party's all over before it begins
You can pour me some Old Whiskey River my friend
But I'll never smoke weed with Willie again

Now we're passing the guitar, we're telling good jokes
I could tell one was coming because I'm smelling smoke
No, I do not partake I just let it pass by
With a grin on my face and a great contact high

I'll never smoke weed with Willie again
My party's all over before it begins

You can pour me some Old Whiskey River my friend
But I'll never smoke weed with Willie again

In the fetal position with drool on my chin
We broke down and smoked weed with Willie again

[Songwriters: Toby Keith and Scotty Emerick]

*"Each time someone stands up for an ideal, or acts to improve the lot of others, or strikes out against injustice, they send forth a tiny ripple of hope, and crossing each other from a million different centers of energy and daring those ripples build a current which can sweep down the mightiest walls*
*of oppression and resistance."*
— Robert F. Kennedy

# 4 LETTERS TO LEADERS

November 20, 2022.   Submission Reference ID: DSV23A5M

Dear Honorable Secretary of Defense Austin and Honorable CIA Director Burns,

I hope it's not too much to ask for your help with a problem I'm having with the CIA Checchi family terrorists. It has to do with the garbage Checchi "data" and cheap tricks / unscientific "eye testing" and psychological games they are playing with me on my computer.

The CIA Checchi terrorists have "developed" very strange, manipulated, biased and unscientific "tests" that are nothing but pure psychological manipulation and more CIA Checchi family nonsense. Since you folks at the CIA train people to do this kind of stuff, I hope I can count on you to right this wrong. What they are doing to me, and thousands of other innocent Americans is unfair and a waste of taxpayer dollars. They are submitting this manufactured "data" to the Supreme Court. Then they get naive or compromised Justices to go along with this garbage "data" as if it is genuine, valid information. This makes a mockery of justice and mockery of the Supreme Court. What they are doing is unjust and nothing but cheap psychological games.

Here's what they are doing: The CIA Checchi family terrorists have "developed" very strange, manipulated, and unscientific "tests" that are nothing but pure psychological manipulation, invasion of privacy, and more CIA Checchi family nonsense.

They are trying to get thousands and thousands of people to look at people's butts & breasts and pet's butts as well. Daily, they plaster social media with hundreds and hundreds of breasts and butt "tests." A person only needs to look at one of these photos for two seconds in order to fail the "test." Sometimes I do look at a butt or someone's chest... because it's perfectly centered in the photo, because it's covered in colorful clothing, because someone is pointing at it, etc. 99% of the time, I'm in my artistic mode looking at a photo or video as a photographer or artist, not looking at the photo as sexual nourishment or inspiration.

With their doctored and fabricated "evidence," they present this "data" as evidence to the Honorable Court that I am sick or sexually preoccupied because I look at these manufactured, manipulated photos for two seconds or more. I'm sure that you know what they are saying is untrue. I can't be the first person to complain about this corrupt terrorist family. I am not able to share links to the hundreds of Yahoo ads that appear on my computer daily, because these ads don't have links. They just pop up on my computer against my will. It's not like I'm clicking on these ads to see more of this fabricated nonsense. I've taken to pasting paper on my computer screen to block from seeing this CIA Checchi family orchestrated nonsense.

For years, these same Yahoo ads have contained information that I needed to know. In other words, people who are "helping me" use these ads to communicate with me. I look at them and try to figure out what hidden message lies within them. I've looked at messages like this for the last ten years because it's how I've been trained to get the information they are giving me. Now to punish me for looking at these same ads and to use this as "data" that I am sick or a sexual pervert... is more Checchi-fabricated nonsense. The Justices are too inexperienced, corrupt, or naïve to understand the games that are being played here. The Checchi's are pure con artists. For example, here is a typical example of what they are putting on my computer to make me look at a butt -
https://twitter.com/thehowie/status/1594501743181807616?s=20&t=mVWDoez13gVCxcMztEw0aw :

Below are some more samples of the kind of nonsense they are plastering on my computer. I bet with the "data" they present, they don't mention how many hundreds and hundreds of photos they are pouring onto my computer.

For example, if I look at 10 or 15 photos in an 8-hour period while I'm working on my computer... they don't mention they put over 200 photos as bait during this time to try and make me look at something. When you realize I only looked at a small percentage of these avalanched photos... the story changes when you realize the small percentage of photos I am looking at as they plaster my computer with hundreds and hundreds of photos EVERY SINGLE DAY.

I bet they also don't mention the high number of accounts I block on my Twitter feed for posting weird and deranged photos. It's not that hard to realize the con artist Checchi family live in a world of pure dishonesty. They are not giving accurate reports of what is truly going on when I am on my computer. They are con artists and scammers 100% of the time. They are not crime fighters. They are terrorists who abuse their power, sexually groom thousands of children, and kill thousands of innocent men, women, and children in America and worldwide.

For example, today is Joe Biden's birthday, and my Twitter feed is full of pics of Joe as a young 19 or 20-year-old guy. Does looking at this photo as it constantly appears on my computer mean I'm a creep? I find it annoying it's constantly appearing on my computer. I can't stop it from appearing. https://twitter.com/BeschlossDC/status/1594435936494010375?s=20&t=qy5Bo1xhoNUMBs6DSTT4ng

Joe Biden is eighty years old today:

4:02 PM · Nov 20, 2022

**2,044** Reposts   **200** Quotes   **30.6K** Likes   **145** Bookmarks

♡        ↻        ♡        🔖 145        ⬆

As for their process being UNSCIENTIFIC: they claim that if I look at a photo for 2 seconds, it is an offense. That's nonsense because it can take you 4 or 5 seconds to even realize what the photo is. Once you realize the photo is a bunch of kids or a bunch of sheep butts... an interested person can decide to click on the photo to get a closer look at something that interests him or her. If I'm not clicking on the photos, I'm not looking at the photo. If it's in my Twitter feed, that means nothing. I am forced to look at everything on my Twitter feed for two seconds. Twitter is where I get 95% of my information from people who are "helping me" during this court case against the

CIA Checchi family. I usually look at every tweet because there are often coded messages for me and information for me that I need to know. Sometimes I have been tricked into clicking on photos or videos that were traps. The Checchi family is out of control, and they need to be stopped because I am not alone in being persecuted and attacked in this way. They are doing this sort of thing to thousands of other innocent people that the Checchi's are framing as creeps or predators.

The Checchi's know how to manipulate me. They have studied me for over thirty years. For example, they know I watch *60 minutes* segments every week. So, this week, they manipulated this segment which, unknown to me, has many children in it: https://twitter.com/60Minutes/status/1594497984624005120?s=20 &t=mVWDoez13gVCxcMztEw0aw

The Checchi's are 100% con artists, and these "eye tests" are more Checchi nonsense that is unscientific and pure garbage data. They manipulated this (and hundreds of other posts with children in them) into my social media feed to make it seem like I'm a creep who is into children. There were no kids in the beginning of this segment or in the advertising of this segment. These are the kinds of tricks the CIA Checchi cult leaders play to set me up as a creep, and they should be fired for playing these games with thousands and thousands of innocent Americans. Unfortunately, they will probably only be charged/fined money for working so hard to tarnish the reputations of thousands of innocent people. In my case, what they are doing is pure retaliation - AGAIN. They have people working very hard to fill my computer with this nonsense. Below are more examples of their deceitful games.

Whatever you can do to right this wrong, I would appreciate your immediate attention. The Justices at the Supreme Court seem to need some help understanding this is a pure Checchi scam. I find it hard to believe Supreme Court Justices with so much education are ignorant about these cheap dollar store tricks of manipulation and deceit.

Thank you for your time and consideration,

Dillon Woods
Independent Journalist

September 27, 2022

Dear CIA Director Burns,

I just caught the CIA Checchi family terrorist cult leaders continuing to attack me and set me up. They are so sneaky! I'm kicking myself because you'd think by now, I'd be hip to their games and manipulations. But I fell for one of their tricks again! I often watch videos on YouTube from a Canadian psychologist named Dr. Jordan Peterson. He recommended that people watch a documentary called *Crumb*.

He said, "*there's a documentary you should watch. I may have mentioned it before. I think it's the best documentary ever made — certainly the best one I've ever seen. It's called, 'Crumb.' It's about an underground cartoonist, Robert Crumb, who was part of the hippie movement — although he hated hippies. He was part of the hippie movement in the 60s in San Francisco and started the entire underground comic culture that manifested itself in graphic novels.*"

So... with such a raving review from a famous internet psychologist, I looked up the *Crumb* documentary and watched it. The entire time I'm watching it, I'm in disbelief that an educated man like Dr. Peterson – a psychologist no less – recommended such crap. Then I realized, this crap is a trap.

There were many short *Crumb* videos that popped up on the YouTube search. All of them were very weird. All of them were another Checchi trap. Apparently, Peterson works for the CIA Checchi cult, and he is helping the Checchi's set people up by sending people to watch these weird videos.

When I watched *Crumb*, they track my "cookies" on my computer, and they will present it as proof I am mentally ill or a criminal/pervert worthy of being killed because I watch things that are creepy and perverted. Here's a clip of Dr. Peterson recommending the video: https://www.youtube.com/watch?v=RvYKBWIPg7E

Psychologists and psychiatrists like Dr. Peterson are among the most dangerous people who are part of the CIA Checchi cult. They have great power to ruin people's lives and even ruin entire families. This abuse of power must be stopped – it's un-American.

Sincerely,

Dillon Woods
Independent Journalist

# 5 MORE CIA CHECCHI FAMILY TRICKS AND TRAPS

MORE CHECCHI TRICKS AND TRAPS PUTTING BUTTS IN MY TWITTER FEED:

Her butt is featured prominently in this video, and it appears on my Twitter feed constantly - https://twitter.com/keithedwards/status/1594370077230600199?s=20&t=zjOKtUCxp-uULJQ-O3GbRA :

Re-sharing this queen today and going to borrow from her strength and fierceness.

A dark photo that takes longer to realize … it's another Checchi trap with young dudes - https://twitter.com/lexyhwhite/status/1594467210072051713?s=20 &t=zjOKtUCxp-uULJQ-O3GbRA :

Chatted with @TXT_bighit at the @AMAs for @TODAYshow

6:06 PM · Nov 20, 2022

**5,141** Reposts   **464** Quotes   **14.9K** Likes   **275** Bookmarks

275

## EYE TESTING WITH VIDEOS ON YouTube, MORE CIA CHECCHI FAMILY NONSENSE

Have you ever wondered how some of these YouTube creators get paid so much money? I have an answer to that question: they are helping the CIA Checchi family cult leaders create content that frames people (sets them up) as creeps by editing their programs in ways that are manipulative and sexualizing.

In this video titled, "I sent robot forgeries to a handwriting expert" we see an example of how manipulative these people can be. In this video, the creator puts a picture of himself as a young teenager (at 1 min 40-45 seconds into the video) and he strategically places text that you are supposed to read over the picture of the young teen. If you read the text, he pulls away the text just in time for the viewer to

57

realize... now you are looking at the young teen's nipples in the shirtless pic of himself as a young teen. I am not posting a screen shot of this because it involves a picture of a young teen.

These are the kind of cheap tricks that the CIA Checchi spies create to trap people... because this is how they make money finding "creeps" as they "test" your eyes and what people are looking at on the computer. This is nothing but pure psychological manipulation and editorial manipulation.

If they are testing your eyes and you read the text in that box on the screen you would be forced to look at the teen's nipples and this would give you a big fat "F" for failing their test. This, of course, is a complete CIA Checchi scam to trap Americans and one way they make money from complete junk science. There are many "creators" on social media involved in creating such traps for unsuspecting viewers. They are con artists, and my opinion is... this video is another set up to frame innocent Americans - orchestrated by someone who most likely is part of the CIA Checchi family cult:

https://www.youtube.com/watch?v=cQO2XTP7QDw&list=TL PQMjcwNTIwMjMhw1I0hgl-0A&index=204.

Not that more proof is needed to make a case that these CIA Checchi cult leaders are corrupt and deceitfully manipulative... but... the CIA Checchi terrorists had this next video appear in my YouTube feed. At 13 seconds in this video at the link below, there is a butt that appears and it's the only thing in the shot. If you look at this butt, you fail the test. Good luck -
https://www.youtube.com/watch?v=yA4tueqAqbI&list=TLPQMjg wNTIwMjPanOL-PTVnFA&index=209 :

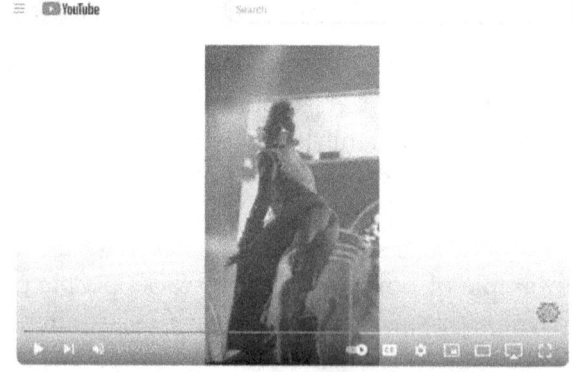

In this music video the editor wastes no time 40 seconds into the video focusing on Lukas Nelson's butt. Checchi spies are compensated for putting up these kinds of videos so they can be used for the CIA Checchi cult's "eye testing" program. These are the kinds of videos that constantly show up in my YouTube feed. It's more complete manipulated nonsense from America's leading con artist group: The CIA Checchi family terrorist cult - https://www.youtube.com/watch?v=dHuuXH1zBTc&list=PLt_L-ABqnN-k_9i4ni2XxBADCImfkKw5g&index=462 :

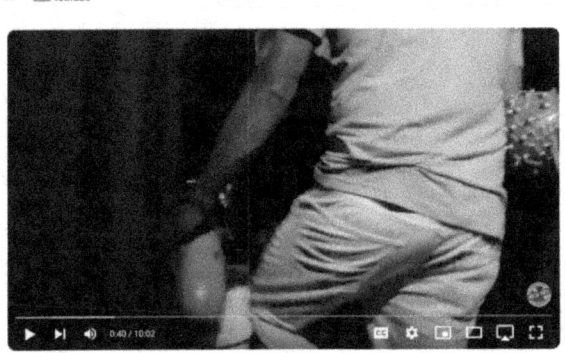

Another annoying video manipulation that is an obvious CIA Checchi editing stunt is here at 10:30-34: https://www.youtube.com/watch?v=zfaAf7kpFdc&list=PLt_L-ABqnN-k_9i4ni2XxBADCImfkKw5g&index=693

The editing trick focus' on the lady's private parts when she closes the drawer. There is no reason that they need to focus on her vaginal area in this shot... except for the fact that they are using this video as bait to frame people and set them up as creeps:

Another CIA Checchi trick can be seen in this video at 1:13-19: https://www.youtube.com/watch?v=WlK4lPS8EZw&list=TLPQM TIwNzIwMjOHFfi9aUdQYQ&index=7

Here they force you to look at the crotch of Elvis by pointing it out and doing a close-up of his crotch. These people have no shame and there is no end to the games they will play to set someone up as a pervert or creep while they are doing their "eye testing" nonsense:

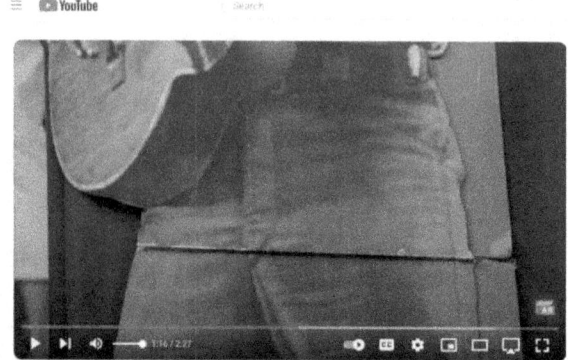

The people who orchestrate, edit and film "Antiques Road Show" seem to clearly, at times, be helping the CIA Checchi cult with their nonsense "eye testing" project. There are so many examples of this nonsense on this show, I can't list them all. But in this link at 2 minutes and 2 seconds: https://www.youtube.com/watch?v=SChI22hTzRg&list=TLPQMT YwNzIwMjN6EYvJdK6LSg&index=4 you'll see a butt prominently displayed next to the art object being talked about. This kind of thing happens so often on this show, it's hard to believe that it's just a coincidence.

If you watch the lady speaking at the 39 second spot, all of the sudden, a butt pops up right next to her head: https://www.youtube.com/watch?v=3-ELFXxJOu4&list=TLPQMTkwNzIwMjO4lwjcIeHW5w&index=11.

This is a typical CIA Checchi trick made to manipulate the viewer's attention through clever editing manipulation - more "eye testing" nonsense.

Why should Americans be concerned about these unethical tricks being played on computers and televisions? The American government is talking about bringing more internet into rural America. Why? Because they play these "eye testing" games and make more money (billions of dollars) framing people as perverts who look at people's butts in video clips such as this one. This "eye testing" program is a massively unjust program because it is built on assumptions and presumptions without sufficient evidence or proof. Simply looking at a body part, does not mean someone is a creep sexualizing that person. Some people are observant, and they study every detail of a video or photo. Assuming that people are sexualizing while they are watching something is a huge assumption. Someone could be looking at any number of things when they look at a body part: They could be looking at the clothing and how it fits on the person; they could be looking at the style of the pockets on the back of the pants; they could be thinking about the fitness level of the person and their body fat percentage. There are many things they could be thinking about besides sex when they look at someone's butt or any body part. It should be a crime for government agents to engage in this nonsense.

I keep finding YouTube Channels that are made by people who are part of the Checchi cult. They deliberately make videos featuring shady moments and inappropriate tricks, meant to make someone look at something inappropriate.

For example, this is a YouTube channel that reviews Checchi movies. The narrator even reviews movies he hates – like Mel Gibson movies – because Mel Gibson is part of the Checchi cult, and the real goal of this review channel is to high light and promote Checchi cult members and Checchi cult movies.

At 5 min 30 sec in this video at the link below the narrator shows a family photo of himself with his Scottish family at the age of 14 years old. He mentions he's wearing a Scottish man's kilt, which of course, makes you look at the kilt. But in the eye testing program, if an adult looks at a teen for more than two seconds it is a failure of the test. You'd get a big fat "F" because the viewer is looking at the kilt which is also in the area of the teen's genitals. This is complete manipulative Checchi nonsense and is more proof the entire eye testing program is more Checchi undue influence and even a form of entrapment:

https://www.youtube.com/watch?v=ojBwASARAzo&list=PLt_L-ABqnN-k_9i4ni2XxBADCImfkKw5g&index=472

For over five decades, the CIA Checchi family has created and manipulated movies in Hollywood to use movies as a communication tool for their network of spies. In 2023 they boast that their network of spies surpasses 500 million+ people who are part of their cult worldwide. Since 2016 the Checchi's have tried to get me to watch the Spiderman movie with Tom Holland, which I resisted because I try to avoid anything they want me to watch.

In 2023 I decided to watch this Spiderman movie and see what all the fuss was about because they keep telling me to watch it. This was another CIA Checchi trap. In the movie he plays the part of an underage teenager, and the movie takes place in a high school. In the first few minutes of the movie, he's basically naked, in his skimpy underwear. This is pure CIA Checchi family creepy manipulation as they try to influence and manipulate people to look at a virtually naked teenager. When you watch the movie on your computer, they have built-in cameras that track the viewers eyes. They are using movies like this to create "evidence" that people are perverts and predators. Even though Tom Holland is not a teenager in real life when he played this role of Spiderman, they have manipulated it so that the viewer still gets an "F" for looking at a virtually naked teenager for more than two seconds. The movie script says he's a teenager. Since everything is being recorded via these computer cameras, they store this "data" as evidence. And by creating this scenario, they get paid millions of dollars as they create a mechanism that collects "evidence" of thousands of people who are all the sudden looking at Tom Holland in his skimpy underwear. Eventually the CIA Checchi family cult leaders make billions of dollars killing people who are a threat to the community and if you are an adult that is looking at virtually naked teens in their underwear – you are a threat to the community. This kind of unethical manipulation is dishonest. It is more CIA Checchi family abuse of power and manipulative undue influence nonsense.

Another series of shows that Oprah Winfrey and the CIA Checchi cult clearly manipulated is when they created sexually explicit scenes with "underage kids" (again, it's possible these actors were not underage when they filmed these scenes) in a series of shows called "Tyler Perry's The Oval." They even have one of the "kids" appearing in multiple scenes completely naked and in one scene, he's masturbating under a restaurant table. HIGHLY suggestive and sexually manipulative nonsense in which Oprah and the Checchi's are making millions of dollars setting up Americans as perverts and child predators.

In this particular show, they are not just framing and setting up any Americans... because this show is on BET – Black Entertainment Television. They are focused on setting up black people. This is another racist attack – targeting people in the black community. I've never seen a show so sexually explicit with "underage" kids (I put it in parenthesis because I suspect the actors are over the age of 18, playing underage characters.). With the teen male character, they glorify a serial-killing teen who is also a masturbation fiend as he masturbates in public, under a table in a restaurant and also in front of his psychologist during a therapy session (then throws his semen on her). In season 2, episode 9 they even have the teen masturbating in front of a White House staffer and camera angle tries hard to virtually show him doing it. This show is a deliberate sexually manipulative program, meant to bring in millions (if not billions) of dollars for Oprah and the CIA Checchi family cult leaders as they use this show as part of their "eye testing" program.

Not everything the CIA Checchi cult leaders use to trap and frame people is a deliberate, calculated creation. Sometimes things just happen spontaneously (like these clips of animals on the David Letterman Show) and they are methodical about putting all these brief animal butt segments into one video. Once they find video they can exploit for their "eye testing" program, they make sure this video appears at the top of people's YouTube feed. Here are a couple examples of more manipulated nonsense the Checchi's do to make someone look at butts – even animal butts -
https://www.youtube.com/watch?v=xgOKX5cQlEs&list=TLPQMj lwNjIwMjNBuVtrFBv_CQ&index=273 :

At 0:23 seconds into the video at this link above, you have a monkey sniffing a dog's butt:

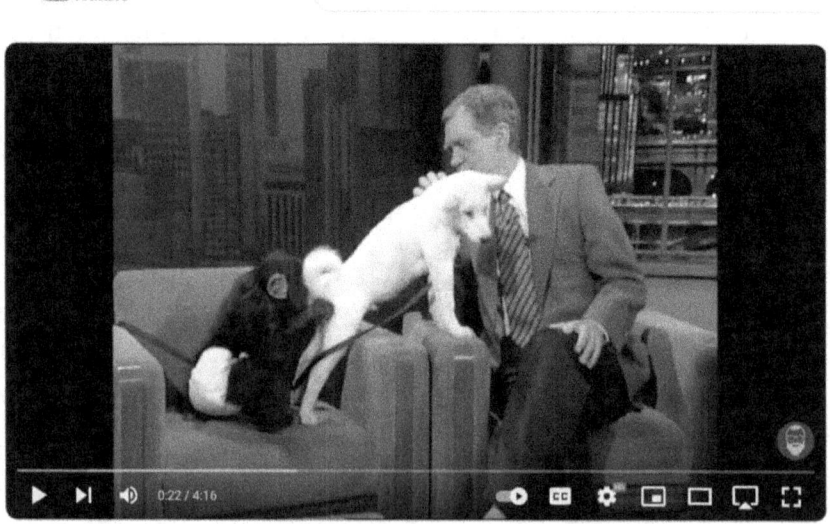

The Best of "Jungle" Jack Hanna | Letterman

At 0:46 seconds the guest ripped his pants, and he makes sure to show the viewers the hole in his pants:

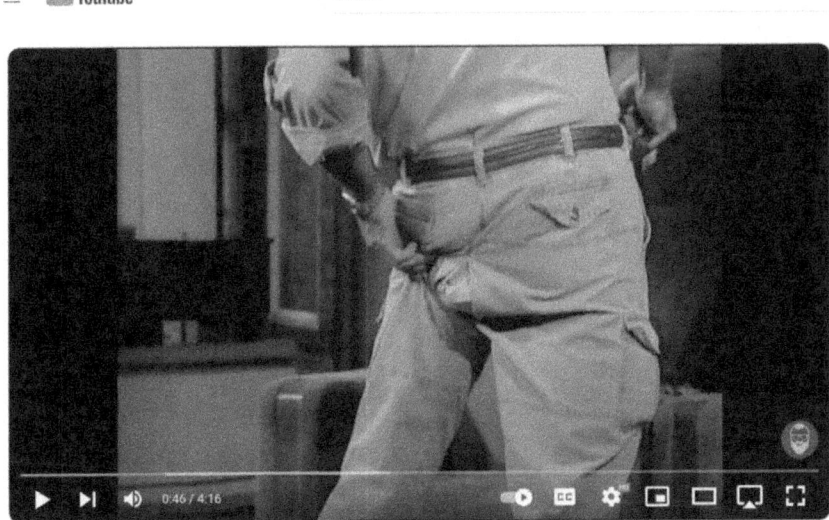

The Best of "Jungle" Jack Hanna | Letterman

At 1:13 you have a skunk's butt being put on display:

The Best of "Jungle" Jack Hanna | Letterman

In this YouTube video they created (at 7 min and 15 seconds), you will see they purposely put a child's butt featured center screen as kids build a tree house. It couldn't be more pronounced and obviously manipulative. This is what they do to "trap" people and set up gullible, naïve people. They say this proves someone is a creep. This is more junk Checchi-science "data" -
https://www.youtube.com/watch?v=1SqlBHT7zYA&list=TLPQMj
EwNDIwMjO4WjE-OBzGLw&index=251 :

15 Stunning Treehouses you'll want to live in

Maluma - COCO LOCO – music video

At 14/15 seconds in the beginning of this music video (no doubt orchestrated by a CIA Checchi cult member) they feature a woman's butt central in the shot. Where else is a person going to look when the previous ten seconds you are manipulated to look only at the center of the screen… which shifts quickly for 2 seconds to this female butt. This is another example of pure psychological and editorial manipulation that the CIA Checchi family uses to set people up for "F" failing grade in their dishonest, manipulated and unethical "eye testing" program:
https://www.youtube.com/watch?v=A4t47LowHyc&list=TLPQM
DgwNjIwMjNyI7vAdcXLxg&index=403

Maluma - COCO LOCO (Official Video)

Even in the most obscure videos (this one is called, *15 LARGEST Fruit and Vegetables*) they put a butt shot in my YouTube feed every day as a way of attacking me and setting me up for an "F" in their nonsense "eye testing" unethical data collection program. Check out this video at 5:03-5:04 – a two second shot will give anyone watching an "F" for looking at this guy's butt...

https://www.youtube.com/watch?v=kw4W-N5Vgjo&list=PLt_L-ABqnN-k_9i4ni2XxBADCImfkKw5g&index=532 :

15 LARGEST Fruit and Vegetables

The movies that the Checchi's make are full of set ups that make the viewer look at people's butts, crotch, and breasts. For example, in *Men in Black: International*. There are many "tricks" they implement in this movie which amount to classic Checchi scams in their "eye testing" program. From naked alien butts to snakes coming out of a

67

guy's back side.

- https://www.youtube.com/watch?v=VWU_tmdxa_g :

For example, at 18:21 a snake comes out of a guy's back side... forcing the viewer to look at his butt. This is a typical Checchi trick that can "count" against someone they are "grading" with their scam of "eye testing."

1:15:50 "Why are you wearing pink trousers" … in the next shot, makes the viewer look at his butt in the pink trousers because his butt is the first thing that appears on screen.

37:37 there is a song playing at this club and the words fully promote sex and drugs with underage teens. This is typical subliminal CIA Checchi family mind control and psychological undue influence. *"Only 13 … dimes wall to wall in the VIP… The age don't mean a thing. I ain't Chi Ali. I bring them out with no ID… come here girl… let me creep in your world…"*

# 6 MORE CIA CHECCHI FAMILY TRICKS AND TRAPS ON SOCIAL MEDIA: CHILDREN, ANIMALS, MILITARY EXPLOITATION

EXPLOITING CHILDREN ON SOCIAL MEDIA:

If you're a spy and you want to attack someone, putting photos of children in their social media feed can be a way to make them appear to be into children. If you can frame someone as a child predator, you can get them killed. Exploiting children and students who are athletes is a favorite obsession, trick, and trap orchestrated by the CIA Checchi family. In this first example, they put an adult athlete with his childhood photos as an athlete:

https://twitter.com/realmadrid/status/1594249372711223297?s=20&t=qy5Bo1xhoNUMBs6DSTT4ng :

In this example, they have an entire team of young ladies taking off their religious garb to play basketball.
https://twitter.com/GEsfandiari/status/1594242676269977600?s =20&t=mVWDoez13gVCxcMztEw0aw :

There is no shortage of military butts that show up on Twitter…
https://twitter.com/StrikeBCT/status/1590367186429759488?s=20
&t=Vey4PLdLFo-u3fonVZ2-jQ :

**Mid-week Mortars!** @StrikeBCT @101stAASLTDIV @VCorps
@FORSCOM @USArmyEURAF

10:34 AM · Nov 9, 2022

**7** Reposts   **47** Likes   **1** Bookmark

Animal butts fill Twitter as well… this is an animal hiding
backwards in a coffee cup.
https://x.com/buitengebieden/status/1580434610399326209?s=20 :

A panda showing his butt off -
https://x.com/buitengebieden/status/1545508914170667008?s=20 :

A Corgi showing his butt off -
https://twitter.com/favcorgi_usa/status/1591750986108108800?s=2
0&t=W6MyPUczIE5JS1REXsqI0Q :

I'm sexy and I know it

6:13 AM · Nov 13, 2022

They even have a Twitter channel dedicated to butts -
https://x.com/butt/status/1674553923074678784?s=20 :

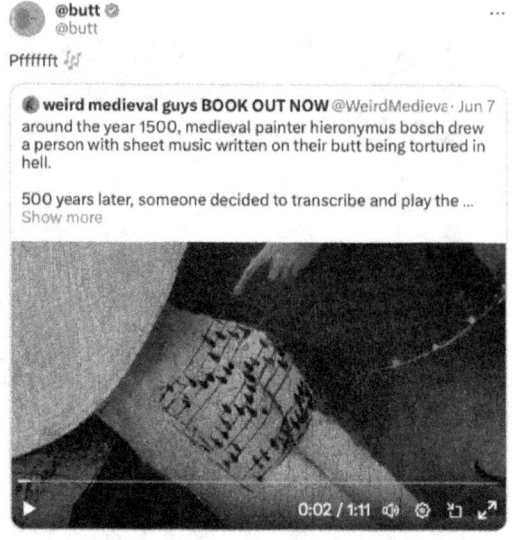

Catia from Sweden is one of the CIA Checchi cult leaders. She likes to send me cat butts on Twitter - https://twitter.com/catturd2/status/1592602588561563648?s=20&t =Na0lZLBxOlPLgw_zdQ7w8g :

This Butt is the only thing showing as you try to figure out what the video is about:

Butts have a constant presence on social media -
https://twitter.com/jakewhomst/status/1587136622058909696?s=2
0&t=EGApmYzrWGuy-z8chRYSPQ :

A group of butts climbing stairs-
https://twitter.com/ValaAfshar/status/1587149813690384384?s=20
&t=EGApmYzrWGuy-z8chRYSPQ :

More suggestive nonsense -

Demings!!! WINNING 😈 #vote #staceyabrams

11:22 AM · Oct 31, 2022

## More butts of young people -

albums of 2002:brooklynvegan.com/35-best-emo-po...

8:59 AM · Oct 31, 2022

I'm sorry Paul I don't believe you or the press!!!!

More butt abuse -
https://twitter.com/RobertJohnDavi/status/1586877093266219010?s=20&t=XdtX9TsxP0UIHSUmy582hA :

8:25 PM · Oct 30, 2022

More breast nonsense even with President Biden involved -
https://twitter.com/realDailyWire/status/1587182007016194050?s=
20&t=XdtX9TsxP0UIHSUmy582hA :

The creepiest part of Halloween is this video

0:06 / 0:08

From **Ian Miles Cheong** ✓

4:37 PM · Oct 31, 2022

Hundreds of these suggestive photos flood social media -
https://twitter.com/rbisrb/status/1587942527579070464?s=20&
t=7RPOCE0S0WNK0dWhxFgBNQ :

Future Husband of Marjorie Taylor Greene.
Voted "Most Likely to Shoot His Pecker Off in High School".

**NOT YOUR FATHER'S GOP**

6:59 PM · Nov 2, 2022

Nakedness in Times Square -
https://twitter.com/leezeldin/status/1587849329477267457?s=20&t
=GO5HmWP-6E1HOVP7zRBXQQ :

SPOTTED in Times Square!

12:49 PM · Nov 2, 2022

They even promote butts on the sports page. There's no reason to
publish a picture like this in a newspaper...
https://twitter.com/GreenwichTime/status/15919546435206963
20?s=20&t=G_oAok0tgCQG8xjuQbI40Q :

The Checchi's are 100% con artists, and these "tests" for the "eyes" of citizens is more Checchi nonsense that is unscientific and pure manipulated garbage.

In their attempt to fill my Twitter feed with young people, here is another example of their manipulated nonsense - https://twitter.com/MerrittForTexas/status/1595597559237693444?s=20&t=J2iDEkCIQGsHs7FvCWnZBg:

8:57 PM · Nov 23, 2022

This video shows a very talented kid playing with a soccer ball. The CIA Checchi family often use talented kids in every sphere (music, sports, etc.) to trap people into watching videos with kids in them. This *"video has a powerful psychological effect on the viewer, drawing them in and capturing their attention due to its captivating nature. The rhythmic movements and mesmerizing tricks performed with the soccer ball create a hypnotic or entrancing effect that keeps the audience engaged and focused on the video."* (ChatGPT 2023)

https://twitter.com/Bakari_Sellers/status/1595566605160906753?s=20&t=rLwZ585TluvhBOrdKbo9dg :

6:54 PM · Nov 23, 2022

More CIA Checchi family exploitation of children, using social media with kids to frame people as child predators or creeps:

The screen on my computer allows me to view 3, 4, 5, 6, 7, or 8 social media posts at one time (depending on how much room the post takes when they add a photo, video, etc.). The Tweet from Buzz Feed (at the link below) is very interesting. It's a 3 minute 39 second video that has five ideas on "5 Zero-Waste Cleaning Product Refills." This is the kind of video that the CIA Checchi family knows I would probably stop and watch a video like this: (https://twitter.com/BuzzFeedFood/status/1595590428417482753?s=20&t=bvmei_HEKo1Ol8iQK8UwoQ).

The CIA Checchi family cult leaders have the ability to manipulate the details of what shows up in my social media and in what order these things appear. Placed directly below this Buzz Feed Tweet is another Tweet which featured a tragic story about a Jewish family in which they feature children. The CIA Checchi family routinely attack people in the Jewish community, so I always take note of terrorism and murders that involves any Jewish people. Placing these two Tweets next to each other is another Checchi trick that manipulates "data." Because I spend almost 4 minutes watching the Buzz Feed video, the Checchi family cult leaders can falsely claim that I spent this time looking at the social media post that had a picture of children (the Jewish family photo features a picture with children). But what I was actually doing during that 3 minute and 39 second time period was watching the Buzz Feed video. Since the two social media posts were next to each other, they can claim I was preoccupied with this photo with children in it:

https://twitter.com/RationalSettler/status/159553539320996249 6?s=20&t=bvmei_HEKo1Ol8iQK8UwoQ

4:50 PM · Nov 23, 2022

This next social media post below is another sinister manipulation, in my opinion. Look at the dad's face on the sofa (he happens to be a public figure and probably a CIA Checchi spy deliberately posting this photo for their "eye testing" program). The dad's face is next to the kid's butt prominently featured to the right of his face, behind him. This sort of photo is typical CIA Checchi family manipulation, abuse of power and ridiculous nonsense trying to get people to look at a kid's butt (which is a serious violation in the "eye testing" program):

1:22 PM · Nov 27, 2022

The Checchi's frequently exploit high school & college football video in order to trap people with their "eye testing" program. Football lends itself to being used frequently because the athletes are physically fit and are often bent over (highlighting their butts) at the scrimmage line before the ball is snapped and the play begins. I don't follow football on my social media feed, yet high school and college football videos keep showing up because it's being manipulated. https://twitter.com/wynstonw_/status/1596343769435181057?s=20&t=D6Kj-krUKfHZZvAtm56b5A :

This is an example of one of the CIA Checchi family's favorite tricks: They put writing on a shirt at or above the chest area to get people to look at a woman's breasts. This writing on her chest will make someone look at her breast area for two or more seconds and this will be a violation in the eye testing program - https://twitter.com/Stonekettle/status/1596528483169144834?s=20&t=SIa4MMnEgV4ZAQadMeESGA :

It is a violation in the "eye testing" program to even look at a dolls butt such as the one in this photo -
https://twitter.com/sovietvisuals/status/1596664371480088576?s=20&t=i_KRmMnrJA-d1JllGcilJw :

More animal butt nonsense -
https://twitter.com/CincinnatiZoo/status/159691212952922931 2?s=20&t=c0HcINwnp5weAuGBkbD4qA :

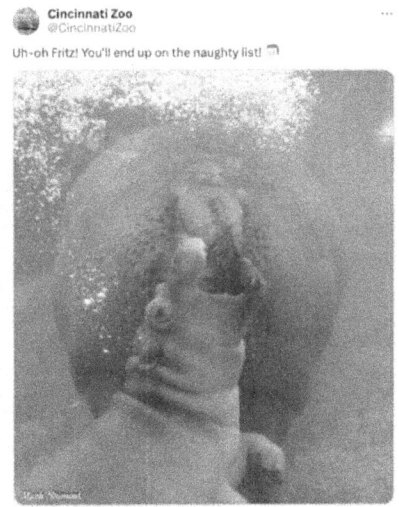

More crotch nonsense is even manipulated in cartoons - https://twitter.com/TheTNHoller/status/1597783237992251393 ?s=20&t=rn47x--bk6X6wDgATH-pwQ :

(H/T @NewYorker)

*"You've literally watched one game."*

9:43 PM · Nov 29, 2022

Even the Mormons are playing penis Checchi games. Why would someone put a dangling necklace that is the shape of a penis at the penis level? Obviously, this was done on purpose.

https://twitter.com/ChristoffDTodd/status/15955490681047654 42?s=20&t=Cy-intIcgjJhkgOwwatczQ :

I was honored to represent The Church of Jesus Christ of Latter-day Saints yesterday at The World Peace Dome in Pune, India as a statue of the Prophet Joseph Smith was added to this majestic hall built to promote world peace.

The CIA Checchi family cult is very involved with NASA. They even get NASA people to play these butt games and support this unethical "eye testing" program. Here is one of the NASA people showing her butt at the end of this video -
https://twitter.com/NASA_es/status/1595784220512772096?s=20&t=zjsZTbISaHjmBSZkcKiBCw :

**Acción de Gracias desde la Estación Espacial Internacional**
Los miembros de la Expedición 68 de la Estación Espacial Internacional, incluyendo al astronauta de origen salvadoreño Frank Rubio, les desean un feliz Día De Acción de Gracias 2022.

9:19 AM · Nov 24, 2022

This video features with opening shots of dancers (0:37 seconds), but the camera is only focused on the breast area of these female dancers. Why not focus on the colorful dresses? This video is another Checchi manipulation scam -
https://www.youtube.com/watch?v=kvBDYwMa7ss&list=TLPQMjMwNTIwMjMt4OLvmOQ6QA&index=229 :

Another common, cheap CIA Checchi family trick is in this video. If you read the words that come up on the screen, they make you look at his pelvic area and his butt because he keeps turning around- complete nonsense "data."

https://twitter.com/jerryteixeira/status/1599069520513368064?s=20&t=wi9nSDaTg8lpN30qo8xXwg :

10:54 AM · Dec 3, 2022

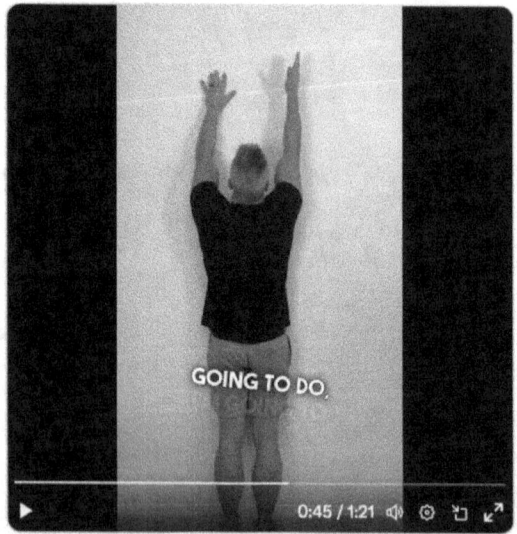

10:54 AM · Dec 3, 2022

More "made you look at a butt" nonsense -
https://twitter.com/metrotimes/status/1599239614241423360?s
=20&t=PwaW1nDX3_br59vffnS0Tg :

Detroit Metro Times
@metrotimes

Things got heated at the Hot and Bothered preview for The Dirty
Show [NSFW PHOTOS]
ow.ly/C22y50LUaEl

10:10 PM · Dec 3, 2022

The lengths that the CIA Checchi family drunks and druggies go to
.... to manipulate people to look at butts on social media -
https://twitter.com/WJCLibrary/status/1599618182079082497?s
=20&t=JRONP1E9_W7MOFFTiVCfxg :

The National Archives @UkNatArchives · Dec 1, 2022
An unexpected visitor has been found rummaging through our
archive boxes this morning

#ElfOnAShelf

ALT

11:14 PM · Dec 4, 2022

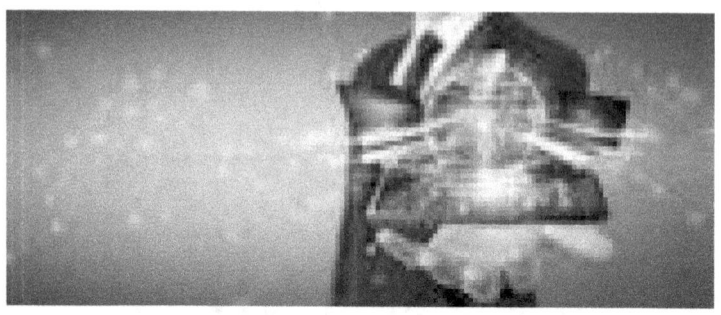

# 7 COMPUTER COOKIES &
# MANIPULATED PHOTOS AND VIDEOS

In any typical business situation, anyone who has been caught being knowingly deceitful and willfully committing fraud would have lost credibility and lost their job a long time ago – but not in the CIA or the military when it comes to the CIA Checchi family. The CIA Checchi family cult leaders have been caught lying, manipulating, invading the privacy of countless Americans, and fabricating "data" for thousands and thousands of innocent people. They have been caught paying "witnesses" to lie in court, they have been caught making photoshopped photographs of people doing illegal things, making "deep fake" videos of people committing crimes, and even blackmailing, bribing, and bullying judicial leaders to force them to give their support to their con artist scams. This includes involving the highest-level political leaders in Congress, the Senate, the Supreme Court and even the White House (both President Biden and President Trump have participated in these CIA Checchi family scams). I don't understand why the CIA Checchi family cult leaders continue to have credibility as they always fabricate and manipulate data they present.

They have been constantly -daily- drunk and simultaneously shooting up heroin, smoking crack, snorting cocaine, smoking crystal meth, and popping pills WHILE THEY ARE WORKING. At the same time they are partying, they have been attacking scores of innocent Americans – accusing these citizens of completely fabricated or exaggerated nonsense. I've never heard of anyone not getting fired for being drunk or high on drugs at work… until now in this situation with the CIA Checchi family. When Ronald Regan said, "*The nine most terrifying words in the English language are: I'm from the government, and I'm here to help…*" he was talking about people like the CIA Checchi family and those who enable them to continue working as government agents after such ridiculous, illegal, and dangerous behavior – spanning DECADES!

The whole CIA Checchi family situation has been a drunken circus enabled by brutal, constant murders of children and other innocent people. It's unfair and it's un-American to allow CIA Checchi family fraud and terrorism to continue to torture and abuse Americans. Enough is enough.

For example, with their "eye testing" program they are saying that people who are looking at these manipulated photos or videos for two seconds or more are guilty of some sort of crime, sickness, mental disorder, or flaw of character. Whatever the CIA Checchi family cult leaders are saying about this "eye testing" program is more complete nonsense, more distortions of truth and more Checchi fabricated lies meant to undermine American democracy and destroy the lives of innocent people. At the same time, they are reaping billions in financial profit for their network and the politicians who help them.

Not only are they lying, manipulating, exaggerating, and fabricating "data" – they know they are doing these things. It is willful fraud! This is a big game to them in which they are making hundreds of billions of dollars. The CIA Checchi family terrorist network has a foundation and culture of constant deceit. They cannot be trusted and must not be allowed to continue this circus of abuse and manipulation.

It is complete nonsense when the Checchi's accuse Americans of "crime," "bad intentions," or "bad character," when naïve citizens look at manipulated photos and videos that involuntarily pop up/appear on their computer screen or a social media feed. In most cases, people are not even clicking on these photos or videos to take a closer look at them. These photos and videos literally appear and disappear from social media feeds via an algorithm that the Checchi's have created. It's not something people control, ask for, or consent to having on their computer screen. I've seen for myself that on websites like Yahoo and other email websites, some very strange things materialize and vanish like there's a digital ghost making things appear and disappear.

On most social media sites, it is possible to block and mute people who post offensive or strange things on your feed. That is not possible to do with the many nonsense ads that appear on Yahoo or other email service websites.

Furthermore, on this subject: The Checchi's often can trick people into looking at a photo or video because they study people and even psychologically profile them. After studying someone, they know what catches the attention of the people they have studied and what interests them. It might be bright colors in a photo or video, movement of any kind, physical fitness, beauty of any kind (human or otherwise), symmetry of any kind (human or otherwise), animals, flowers, gardening, cooking, etc. They know how to manipulate certain reactions from people.

Furthermore, when someone looks at a photo or video, there is no direct line into someone's brain about what they are thinking. For example, to assume the person is thinking something sexual when looking at someone's butt or chest is totally ridiculous and very immature – this is bad science and bad assumptions.

I've noticed the Checchi's have put a lot of animal butts on my computer. These butts are usually centered perfectly on the computer screen. I have not studied the psychology of manipulating people's attention in photographs and videos. But, centering it perfectly on the screen has something to do with being able to manipulate people to look directly at whatever they are trying to get someone to focus on. There is a psychology and science to all this CIA manipulation nonsense. Then using these manipulated videos and photos as "evidence" against someone takes it all to a new level of diabolical. The fact that they are creating these manipulation programs with tax-payer money is unacceptable.

According to ChatGPT (2023): *"The psychological manipulation of directing attention in photographs or videos to specific focal points is often referred to as visual attention manipulation or attentional bias. It involves techniques or compositional elements deliberately used to guide the viewer's gaze towards particular areas of an image or video.*

*There isn't a specific psychological term that exclusively describes the act of directing attention to certain body parts, such as centering a butt or breasts in a photograph. However, this type of manipulation often falls within the broader field of visual perception and psychology.*

*Several concepts and techniques are employed to manipulate attention:*

**Composition and Framing:** *Placing certain elements in the center or using leading lines, framing, or contrast can draw attention to specific areas.*

**Color and Contrast:** *Using colors, contrasts, or brightness to highlight specific parts of an image can attract attention.*

**Point of Interest:** *Placing the main subject or a visually striking element strategically within the frame to immediately catch the viewer's eye.*

**Motion and Movement:** *Incorporating movement or using motion cues can guide attention to particular areas in videos.*

**Subtleties in Visual Design:** *Utilizing psychological principles such as the Gestalt principles (like figure-ground relationship or closure) or even the Rule of Thirds to direct attention to specific points.*

*Manipulating attention in visual media relies on exploiting the brain's natural tendencies in perceiving and processing visual information. It involves understanding how humans naturally focus on certain areas or elements in an image or video."*

For many years, the CIA Checchi family terrorists told me to watch certain videos on YouTube. These videos had content with children and things that were sexually suggestive because they were using this "data evidence" to get secret society people to stalk me and attack me. This went on for many years when I was trusting toward the Checchi family, and I was very naïve and gullible. I had no idea what they were doing to turn this "data' against me in an effort to get me killed.

There are people in this country that will kill you for watching the wrong things when you are on your computer. It took me many years to figure out what a mess the Checchi family was creating for my life. If there were a long digital trail of me watching creepy videos or kid videos, secret society people and others who are into this sort of thing would have an "excuse" to attack me and even kill me for being a 'threat to national security.' If they attacked me, this would give the Checchi terrorists ammunition to kill them. That is why it is said there is a war between the CIA and various secret society groups worldwide. They have been using me to draw out secret society people from the shadows for over twenty years. Unfortunately, for many years I cooperated with this CIA Checchi family nonsense – not realizing exactly what they were doing. They told me hundreds of lies to keep me engaged in helping them with this project.

I can tell you for sure that these games to manipulate secret society people into attacking me have gone on for over two decades, and it has affected my health in many negative ways. Constantly moving because of being constantly attacked has given me PTSD, sleepless nights due to nightmares, various forms of declining health and complete isolation without friends or affection is a form of severe psychological torture.

I have had hundreds and hundreds of people who have stalked me with their children and teenagers who all tried to get me to interact with their kids - forcing their kids to talk to me. It has been a horrible thing to witness this abuse of children. One time a kid about ten years old started crying two feet in front of me. He yelled at his father, "I don't want to talk to him. Leave me alone." The Checchi's goal in using me in this way is to get secret society people to show them the next generation of secret society people, so they can be killed. When I realized the Checchi's were killing some of these secret society children, it made me sick. I refuse to be used as bait so that children can be abused and even killed.

The physical assaults, aggressive attacks, and psychological torture I have endured for over two decades has negatively affected my normally cheerful, gracious demeanor when in public. I used to be affable and talk to everyone when I went out in public. In the beginning, I had no idea it was all a trap that the CIA Checchi family was setting for me. This torture and abuse of power have ruined the nice, approachable person that I used to be. I used to think that a stranger was just a friend I hadn't met yet. This CIA abuse has scarred me permanently on a psychological level. I trust no one anymore and for good reason.

While this has gone on, the Checchi family cult leaders have made over 6 billion dollars using me as bait to draw out secret society people that they eventually killed. For many years, I had no knowledge that they were killing people. I had been told many lies to keep me engaged in this project and producing for them. During this entire time, they did not give me a dime as compensation for working on this project. I had no idea they were making money off me – much less 6 billion dollars. It is beyond ridiculous what unethical government agents are allowed to do to unknowing, gullible citizens.

According to ChatGPT, "*When someone is working for someone else and is not being paid for their labor, this can be a form of human trafficking, specifically a form of labor trafficking. Human trafficking involves the exploitation of individuals through force, fraud, or coercion for various purposes, including labor, sex, or other services.*

*Labor trafficking occurs when individuals are compelled to perform labor or services through force, fraud, or coercion. It can involve various forms of exploitation, such as being forced to work without proper compensation, being threatened with harm, physical violence, or other forms of coercion to keep them in a situation against their will.*

*Not receiving payment for work performed, especially when it's a result of coercion or deception, falls within the realm of labor trafficking. The victims in such situations are often controlled by their traffickers and forced to work under exploitative conditions, with their wages withheld or denied entirely.*

*Labor trafficking is a serious violation of human rights, and it's recognized internationally as a form of modern-day slavery. It exploits individuals and deprives them of their freedom and fair compensation for their work, often under harsh and inhumane conditions.*

*It's crucial to identify and address such situations to provide support and assistance to victims of labor trafficking and to hold accountable those responsible for exploiting and victimizing individuals in this manner. Laws and regulations aimed at preventing human trafficking and providing support to victims are in place in many countries to combat this egregious violation of human rights."*

## ADVERTISEMENTS ONLINE

Recently, I have been looking at the same picture that was part of an ad for a company. It popped up on my computer 30 times a day. The the Checchi's were flashing this ad on my computer so frequency that I was wondering if there is something I am supposed to see in it (a message from them) that I was not understanding. So, I kept looking at the ad and studying it, trying to figure out the message.

It turns out there was no message – this ad was another CIA Checchi family trick trying to trap me. Come to find out... they were just using this advertisement as more "evidence data" to further their narrative about me that I am sick with a mental illness. My only mental deficit is that I'm too trusting, too gullible, and too naïve – I keep falling for these Checchi tricks.

I eventually sued the Checchi's for attempted murder in federal court. I won the case and they appealed to the Supreme Court where a whole different level of corruption and abuse of power took place. It was at the Honorable Court that they presented my entire digital history. These ads, movies, YouTube videos, social media posts are things that they had planted in my life and now used this digital history as "data evidence" that I was a sick person, worthy of being killed. I've written more about this experience in my book, "*Reporting Child Abuse and CIA Abuse of Power.*"

The Checchi's exhibit a high level of expertise in their presentations, but there are concerns about the accuracy and integrity of the data they are providing to the Honorable Court. It appears to be a well-rehearsed process, and there are suspicions that similar tactics might have been used in other cases. Some individuals speculate that certain Justices may not detect the potential issues with the information presented. Additionally, there are allegations that a few Justices might have conflicting interests, which could influence rulings in favor of the Checchi's, potentially undermining the impartiality of the court.

Sometimes, I look at photos for an extended period to discern if the photo has been photoshopped or not. To assume I'm thinking something sexual or perverted is just not accurate. If I find the man in the photo sexually appealing, if I look at his butt and it's in perfect form... what I usually think in my mind is, "that's a lot of work" or "he's worked hard to look that good." Even with sexually appealing men, I find myself thinking of personal training and how much work it takes to look that perfect. I also may just be admiring his beauty. It possible to look at someone who is beautiful and NOT be thinking about sex when you look at them. To assume everyone thinks about sex is childish and incorrect.

The fact that the CIA Checchi family terrorists get paid for manipulated data like this (examples in the links below), is nonsense. This is very far from anything that is genuine data about me. What the Checchi's are doing is inaccurate and not based on genuine scientific methods. What they do is pure manipulation and abuse of power. They tilt the table in their favor. They know what they are presenting is manipulated data, not genuine information.

Animals:
Cat looking at Bird's butt -
https://twitter.com/SlenderSherbet/status/1585704378664685570?s=20&t=pLddVilr3kkNGt8gh1B6Ag :

"What, me? Nothing, I was just checking the wall"

instagram.com/masaki1133

2:45 PM · Oct 27, 2022

In this social media post, they are asking people to please share this video, which is nothing but a corgi's butt, while skateboarding - https://twitter.com/corgitrends/status/1586092260524838912?s =20&t=2tUm9j_HP9HmVu2EAZkvjg :

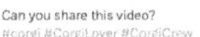

4:27 PM · Oct 28, 2022

There have been an unusually high number of tweets recently appearing on my social media feed involving teens. Videos and pictures that force you to look at certain body parts (butts, breasts, crotch) or photoshopped pics. This video was taken down, so I could not get a screen shot of it. But it was "priceless" because it was used to trap and frame many people -

https://twitter.com/ValaAfshar/status/1586356054941896709?s=20&t=_fh432KfmYSSQGWzVEVB3A :

Violence is a common theme of the CIA Checchi cult. The cult leaders are grooming kids for fighting and violence:

https://twitter.com/MilsteinFF/status/1585928279445319682?s=20&t=HjMgoEim6POi1CX1YxecRg :

UFC lightweight star Natan Levy gave Jewish teenagers in Las Vegas lessons on how to defend themselves

5:35 AM · Oct 28, 2022

Teens fighting - https://twitter.com/2020BestFights/status/158578131498013491 9?s=20&t=gwRgEIowzp7iCk_ra6_SYw :

Murder of 15-year-old indigenous boy - https://twitter.com/AJEnglish/status/1585823546789560320?s= 20&t=K0vDuDKrCzoLq6z3QNIaoQ :

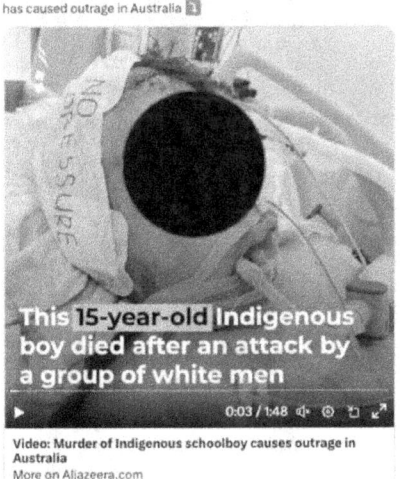

More dog butt nonsense -
https://twitter.com/favcorgi_usa/status/1585933222516785154?s=20&t=udbE1JaM8sTVs0vZhGvqyA :

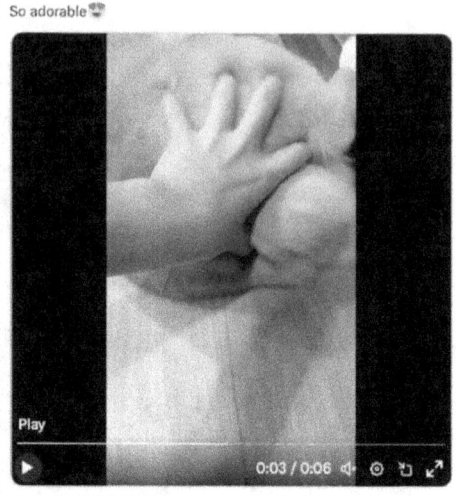

More human butt nonsense -
https://twitter.com/rbisrb/status/1586076655277293568?s=20&t=XLnRRQpw4e7tkDMdsoC37A :

More butt nonsense -
https://twitter.com/WhitlockJason/status/158646184397938278
4?s=20&t=lifXW_QEUcdnQOBymdgksw :

More child and butt nonsense:

https://twitter.com/ValaAfshar/status/1586803623467646976?s
=20&t=aCr5zUhRp1X3Q1s2ns8Ohg :

From **Praveen Angusamy IFS**

3:33 PM · Oct 30, 2022

More with President Biden (I'll let you be the judge of what is being protruded in this video clip):
https://twitter.com/RNCResearch/status/1586904137077489664
?s=20&t=aCr5zUhRp1X3Q1s2ns8Ohg :

10:13 PM · Oct 30, 2022

More boob nonsense:
https://twitter.com/RealLyndaCarter/status/15870859963106426
90?s=20&t=4u4cGyK-ll5oUyvm6qWWLw :

10:16 AM · Oct 31, 2022

This is all more Checchi games of manipulation and deceit. They are lying to the Honorable Court again because they know what they are doing and how they are manipulating and fabricating data.

https://twitter.com/frequentbuyer1/status/1585957867609522176?s=20&t=3DxOO6aiXbdzQ1ZnIm1F_w :

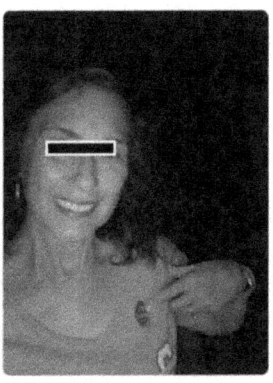

7:32 AM · Oct 28, 2022

## WHAT PEOPLE WATCH ONLINE

There are people who have the job of watching what Americans are watching online. These hidden spies may or may not have good reason to invade someone's privacy in this way. The CIA Checchi family cult leaders generously set traps and tricks on the internet, on televisions, and on social media for thousands and thousands of Americans. From documentaries like the one about Loretta Lynn which is filled with underage teen video shots and storyline of her getting married at age 14 or 13… to a very large amount of porn featuring underage teens on Twitter. Again, these are often situations of pure entrapment and undue influence because the CIA Checchi family cult leaders control the algorithms that bring these videos into someone's social media feed. They also get their spies to influence people to watch things online that they should not be watching as a way to manipulate people they want to set up or frame as predators or creeps. Sometimes, videos will even appear on someone's computer and start playing without even clicking on them. Mysteriously, some people's computers have a ghost in them that make things appear and disappear. This ghost is called CIA CHECCHI FAMILY ABUSE OF POWER.

# 8 SOLUTIONS

What can Americans do to combat this prolific invasion of privacy, entrapment, and undue influence that government agents are allowed to do to unknowing, gullible American citizens?

1. Vote in every election. Do your homework on which candidates believe in the United States constitution, are independent thinkers (not slaves to a corporate donor, fraternal organization, or government agency).
2. Get involved with your elected officials. Write them. Call them. Make your voice heard on issues you care about. Complain when something is going on that you don't like – for example, this 'eye testing" program is a ridiculous example of something that needs to be shut down. It's an invasion of privacy and the CIA Checchi family cult leaders are using these unethical games to frame unknowing, gullible Americans.
3. One of the most important skills a person can learn is discerning who the spies are that have come into your life. There are many kinds of spies and many different portals from which they come. Being able to identify spies will help someone be able to avoid their games. Once you identify a spy you know they will play games with you, and you cannot believe or trust anything they say. Spies can cause all kinds of problems in your life. Identifying who they are early will help you avoid problems. For example, watching shows on the television or the computer with spies can be part of the undue influence or entrapment

they bring into your life. I was too trusting with people I should never have trusted, and it caused a lot of problems in my life. I feel most sorry for the people who are married to a spy, and they don't even know it. These people are very vulnerable to tremendous problems. What these spies do is fraud. Sophisticated, manipulated, unadulterated fraud and people are best to beware and be on guard – your life and livelihood may depend on it.

4. This next idea is not for everyone, but it's worth mentioning: For those who work on the computer or spend a lot of time watching television, wearing sunglasses will help to make it harder for the "eye testing" program to affect your life in a negative way. It will also help to decrease the bright glare of the screen as well.

5. I once heard a news cast that said Queen Elizabeth watched TV on a projection screen. When I first heard this reported in the news I immediately thought, "what a strange thing to report on. What does that mean?" Years later, of course, I came to understand something that she knew: There is an "eye testing" program carried out on modern day TV's and computers all over the world (the CIA is a worldwide organization). There are people watching what you watch and reporting if you spend more than 2 seconds looking at something (like butts and breasts) they think you should not be looking at. And… if you fail this "eye testing" too many times, the consequences are severe, even fatal if they are able to frame you many times.

6. It might be helpful is someone invented a "scrolling option" for all social media sites. We should have a scrolling option where we can set the speed at which we want the social media feed to scroll on the computer screen. This will help keep things moving so that it's harder for the eye testing people to be accurate in their assessments. Most of us just go on social media to find the most recent news. If we had a scrolling option, it might be helpful to end the nonsense of "eye testing." If the social media feed is constantly moving, they can't claim you are looking at something for two seconds or more. If you do want to take a closer look at a post, you click on it and stop the scrolling.

*"Justice delayed is justice denied."*

- William E. Gladstone

# 9 THE SUPREME COURT OF THE UNITED STATES CODE OF CONDUCT

Manipulating the Supreme Court has been a central component of the CIA Checchi family cult leader's success in getting away with prolific criminal activity and crimes against humanity. If it weren't for widespread corruption and certain leaders deliberately ignoring this corruption, the United States wouldn't be in the current mess we find ourselves in.

Thank goodness that on November 13, 2023, the Supreme Court finally agreed to adopt a Code of Conduct for the Justices. I don't have formal legal training to judge the merit of this Code of Conduct, but I do have common sense and three years of experience with a legal proceeding that was at the Supreme Court. If public institutions, like the Supreme Court, move away from a foundation that is established on common sense, that institution no longer serves the common people. It is crucial for the Supreme Court to consistently prioritize the common people's interests in all their actions, including implementing a Code of Conduct.

In my opinion, the new code of conduct for Supreme Court Justices is a very permissive document, written with very accommodating language. Some Americans find this new code to be written in an insulting form because it seems that it was drafted to placate people who have been complaining about the corruption at the Supreme Court for years. If the Justices who drafted this document were serious about ethics and accountability, they would have established ways for people to complain about corruption and would tell more how this new code would be enforced.

Although the code lacks enforcement and complaint procedures, it's a small step in the right direction, despite its limitations. An example of its limitation can be seen when the "suggestion" word "should" appears 54 times in the document. The "obligation" word "must" only appears 6 times in the new code of conduct. It seems someone was very crafty in writing it, which smells slightly of more insincere legal games, if you ask me. Whoever wrote this seems to think people won't perceive this as a problem.

An example of something that must be changed or given more scrutiny is Cannon 3B Section five of the Supreme Court Code of Conduct: *"A Justice should keep informed about the Justice's personal and fiduciary financial interests and make a reasonable effort to keep informed about the personal financial interests of the Justice's spouse and minor children residing in the Justice's household."*

It has been said that in the world of politics and public service, "children are vulnerabilities." This is because one of the first things that bullies and terrorists attack or threaten are the children or grandchildren of the person they want to control. From what I've seen with the CIA Checchi family's bullying of judicial, military, and political leaders, it's not hard to get a public servant to make decisions based on protecting their family rather than protecting what's in the best interest of the public, which they are sworn to serve. President Biden's 2023 Thanksgiving photo with his many grandchildren emphasized these vulnerabilities for him. It makes one wonder if more single people with no children should get involved in politics and public service. Maybe we need more leaders who are not so vulnerable?

The CIA Checchi family cult leaders routinely financially reward/bribe adult children/grandchildren of politicians and justices. Politicians, military professionals, and judicial leaders live in a world where they are mired in CIA Checchi family fear and favor. These leaders fear the serial-killing Checchi family, and the adult children of these public servants live in a world where they often get lucrative jobs – in some cases jobs they aren't trained for, experienced in nor rightly deserve based on many years of hard work. This happens with every single political, military, and judicial professional the Checchi's target – which has been thousands over six decades. Rich people often leave their wealth to their children. The Checchi's skip the inheritance part and give directly to the children while the politician, military leader and judicial professional are still alive. Few things delight a parent more than seeing their offspring do well financially.

Cannon 3B Section five of the Supreme Court Code of Conduct should not be limited to minor children. Corruption seeps into the lives of hundreds of our leader's adult children as a way of rewarding corrupt judges, military professionals, and compromised politicians. Public awareness and action are critical to halt these practices.

For example, once Vice President Harris was in power in January 2021, it was widely reported that Ella Emhoff (VP Harris' stepdaughter) had a new job and was given a modeling contract with IMG Models Worldwide. The news about Jared Kushner being given two billion dollars from the Saudis after he left working for President Trump at the White House as a senior advisor, is another example. The news about Hunter Biden getting a lot of money from a Ukrainian energy company called Burisma Holdings is old news – but it stands as another example. It seems that none of these children of politicians did anything illegal, yet the fact that the CIA Checchi family orchestrates these kinds of 'gifts' for the children of political, military, and judicial leaders must be acknowledged and prevented – otherwise, this is a form of sanctioned bribery, corruption, and inappropriate influence.

I care about this issue because my legal case against the CIA Checchi family has been constantly up against a wall of corruption at the Supreme Court. Justices Thomas, Roberts, Kavanaugh, Alito,

Barrett, and occasionally Gorsuch have often disregarded the rule of law, succumbing to blackmail, bribery, and bullying orchestrated by the Checchi family. There was constant CIA Checchi family fraud and dishonesty over 3 ½ years of judicial corruption. A favorite tactic the Checchi family employed has been orchestrating terrorist events to intimidate Justices, politicians and military leaders who are trying to hold the Checchi family accountable for their lawless behavior.

After yet another bitter fight at the Supreme Court on November 30, 2023, I emerged victorious once again. Shockingly, the very next day, former Supreme Court Justice Sandra Day O'Connor was tragically killed by the CIA Checchi family. This appalling event occurred immediately following a ruling in my favor by the Supreme Court Justices. The murder of Justice O'Connor was a blatant attempt by the Checchi family to intimidate and coerce the Supreme Court into ruling favorably in their ongoing case against me. The Checchi's persist in fabricating 'evidence,' resorting to tactics such as creating deep fake videos, paying witnesses to lie (they are Checchi spies), and producing photoshopped images, all while leveling baseless accusations against me. This act of murder against a retired Supreme Court Justice was a heinous obstruction of justice and an egregious attempt at intimidation.

In Washington, D.C. it is well known among insiders that the CIA Checchi family has experience at killing Supreme Court Justices. The Checchi family cult leaders were 100% involved in killing both Justice Scalia and Justice Ginsberg, which I have already discussed at length in my previous writing (*"Reporting Child Abuse and CIA Abuse of Power"*). If we find some of the remaining Justices at the Supreme Court to be compromised and corrupt, we may want to keep in mind they are only human beings being intimidated by a serial killing family with a license to kill. It would not be a surprise to learn that some of these Justices live in occasional fear for their lives, knowing the serial killing Checchi family can kill any of them or their loved ones at will. The Checchi's have most likely also infiltrated the Supreme Court Police and can manipulate them at will – which is not a comforting reality if you're worried about proper protection for Justices at the highest court in the land. Maybe these Justices are actually very good people in a very difficult situation that has grave consequences? Whatever the case, the American people and leaders in Congress must help them have the guard rails and structure they need to facilitate true justice for everyone – regardless of economic status, education, family ethnicity or pressure from serial killing terrorists, like the CIA Checchi family.

Throughout the nearly four years of my legal battle against the CIA Checchi family cult leaders, I have observed instances where certain Justices at the Supreme Court seem to have allowed these CONVICTED CRIMINALS who are leaders of the CIA Checchi family cult to operate freely, potentially perpetuating further harm and serious crimes against the American people and humanity. These proceedings, conducted in secrecy, raise concerns about accountability and transparency, eroding public trust in the judicial process. There appears to be a perception of corruption that impedes the smooth functioning of justice at the highest level. It feels as though the impartiality symbolized by Lady Justice might have been compromised or obscured in these circumstances, raising questions about the integrity of the system. It seems clear in some instances that Lady Justice has lost her blindfold, or someone stole it from her. Or maybe they gave her free luxury vacation in trade for it?

I'm no legal scholar, but there seems to be one simple solution: Make Supreme Court Justices be duty-bound to the same code that all federal judges must follow. Why can't all federal judges operate under the same code? American citizens and judicial professionals deserve clear and consistent rules of conduct for all judges and Justices.

Sincerely,

Dillon Woods
Independent Journalist

## " *The true administration of justice is the firmest pillar of good government.* " - George Washington

THIS NEXT SECTION HIGHLIGHTS PUBLIC COMMENTS FROM SOME AMERICANS ON SOCIAL MEDIA ABOUT THE CODE OF CONDUCT SHORTLY AFTER IT WAS MADE PUBLIC ON NOVEMBER 13, 2023:

Citizens for Ethics
@CREWcrew
*When transparency and ethics laws are rarely abided by, lifetime appointments encourage outside actors to unethically gain Supreme Court justices' favor using expensive personal gifts, travel and other means. SCOTUS needs to implement term limits.*

Robert Reich
@RBReich
*The Supreme Court's new "Code of Ethics" changes nothing.*
*It has no enforcement mechanism and no mechanism for the public to lodge complaints of misconduct. It's essentially useless.*
*Don't fall for the PR stunt. The court is still living outside the bounds of rules.*
*The Supreme Court's new ethics code is neither a code nor about ethics.*
*It's a pathetic attempt at pacifying the public instead of holding justices accountable.*

Sherrilyn I
*The release by SCOTUS a Code of Ethics is a big deal. Most revealing is the*

*"Statement" that precedes the Code. The insistence that they have only created this b/c so many ppl "misunderstand" their practice is peak gaslighting. It's also the kind of small & begrudging statement that reveals how agonizing this was for some members of the Court. Which means they felt compelled, forced to do something they didn't want to do. Those members wanted to be clear that in their view, THIS IS NOT NECESSARY. And yet the creation of the Code proves they know IT IS.*

*As to the substance of the Code, the words "knowingly" and "knowing" are liberally dispersed, and the changes to how the Code for U.S. Judges defines when a judge's impartiality might reasonably be questioned are telling. And frankly, concerning.*

*Contrast a judge's impartiality might be questioned:*
*Code for U.S. Judges: "when reasonable minds w/ knowledge of all the relevant circumstances disclosed by a reasonable inquiry…."*
*SCOTUS Code: "where an unbiased & reasonable person who is aware of all relevant circumstances…"*
*And there are more differences. Why? The Code that covers other federal judges is adopted after public comment is received on proposed changes. Here the Court arrogated to itself the power & expertise to develop a unique code that differs from that which covers all other judges…*
*…which the Court claims it has been following. So, they "did it." They released a code. But the manner in which it was developed & presented continues the display of arrogance that has brought us to this point. I need to do a side-by-side to see all of the differences w/ the code.*
*But what I've seen is concerning. None of us should be in charge of creating w/o consultation, the ethics rules that will cover our own conduct. The temptation to reverse engineer is too great. Of course, the question of enforceability is paramount. But there are other concerns. A step in the right direction. But a very small step.*

Bobby D
*..no unenforceable code is a big deal.*

Dirk S
*That cover letter absolutely confirms that they don't "get it" and view it as window*

*dressing. I don't really understand how the same members are willing to participate in such a charade.*

Sue
*I mean, what's the problem with accepting bribes, houses, RVs, luxury trips in exchange for some favorable rulings for the bribers?* 🙂

\*Democratic. 📇 ⚖️ us
*And without real consequences for breaking the code, it's more of Clarence on the honor system.*

Emm M
*The whininess of it is very Republican.*

Benj
*Yep, the whole "misunderstanding" thing is a siren.*
*The courts' audience of legitimacy is the people, and their aggregate interpretation of ethical malfeasance supersede historical "established in illegitimacy" institutional carve-outs.*

Jeanne
*What it tells me, and they know it too, is that some members don't belong on the bench. Some of the members' arrogance and unwillingness to step away from rulings, has made their opinions all the more frustrating to Americans. We pay their wages and they play with our lives.*

Standing for Democracy us ♡ ♡
*We didn't know until 2015 that we needed a legally binding ethics code for Presidents either. But we should have. Obviously same with SCOTUS. Power breeds corruption.*

Kleptocracy Now™
*"There's a 'code of ethics' for you. Now shut up and leave us alone so we can on with the grift."*

## Linda P. 'HERE, Truth Matters' 🐾🐾🐾
*It's total bull$hit since there's no consequences for breaking the ethics...which they are all well aware of.*

## Donna C
*Also, it's useless. No way to enforce it.*

## Joel R
*Like children who get caught with their hand in the cookie jar, the court's effort to save face is lame. Thomas' ethical breaches are indefensible but of course he points his finger at others refusing to be held accountable.*

## Janet S
*Tis amazing when SCOTUS justices are victims of misunderstanding.*

## Linne B USIE 🚩☐☐☐☐☐☐☐NOIL
*Four justices that we know of took bribes. BRIBES. And delivered favorable rulings to the oligarchs bribing them. They committed crimes and show their contempt with this weak code of ethics that does nothing to prevent or punish continued behavior.*

## Truthorfiction
*It's the fox guarding the henhouse. Pure theater and useless.*

## Dawn
*Based on what I've learned so far their "code of ethics" is a slap in the face to anyone who cares about the integrity of our courts. It's an attempt to "appear" to do something while doing absolutely nothing to address the massive problems that have been uncovered.*

## Mistsandgrass
*It's insulting is what it is.*
*Do they think that little band-aid covers the stink of their corruption?*

debraj1121

*Unless Congress holds them accountable, nothing will change. Would really like to know that the President is willing to add to the court or set term limits if he ever gets that bill.*

Old Chicago Sunroof

*Damage has already been done.*
*This is disingenuous pandering and won't mean a thing.*
*Real reform removes Thomas, Gorsuch, Kavanaugh and Barrett.*

Judith CL

*A big deal? Peak gaslighting more like.*

Wendell G

*What's the enforcement mechanism in the code?*

Bla-ren

*The Supreme Court has been tarnished, the curtain pulled back. Another failure in this great experiment.*

Gehennan

*I think they don't understand how much they've lost the respect of the bar. Because we absolutely understand their practice, as well as how judicial ethics are supposed to work and how far they have fallen from those standards.*

phillystrong

*Nobody misunderstands.*

JanMP

*It's pathetic. And dishonorable. And weak.*

dean_s🔲UA

*It's increasingly difficult to keep the faith in that so called arc of justice.*

BlackP
*Meh. I'm not as much into a SCOTUS ethics code w/o policing/enforcement mechanism as I am a joint resolution from Congress on what behaviors will result in an impeachment.*
*It would be instructive, however, to review the Abe Fortas case +*
*Nixon/Mitchell dirty tricks re SCOTUSJs.*

Ann D
*INFINITESIMAL step.*

Phil Z
*It is important to remember that it is the Supreme Court that is the real victim here.*

Thomas A
*Pious and pretentious*

Jessica F
*It's a love letter to Dick Durban.*

T. M
*Those with a clue mark the calendar and bring edits to this so it has process, procedures and teeth.*

KDR n' Bear
*This so called code has no teeth! It's the SCOTUS saying these are the rules and we will make sure we follow them. It's* 🐷 💩

Jackie B
*Yes. It's truly a patronizing and defensive attempt to quiet the "little people" who couldn't possibly understand that the SC justices are the most ethical and wise in the land.*

jay's.mom
*Voluntary, and no enforcement. SC doesn't wish to be disturbed in the bubble we provided them.* 🔍 ⍰

John H
*There aren't terms like "shall", or "will" or "must" but only a few milk toast references to "should"*

Gail D B
*Absolutely no enforcement. Just another sham.*

GG Cares
*No way to "misunderstand" the bribery that has been going on for years, and these lovely words do NOTHING to address that, nor prevent it in the future!!*

BEA6119_WeMustDoMoreToHelp ☮
*Dear CJR—I did not misunderstand. Thank you.*

Shawn O
*Congress has the power to pass a law that says they follow the exact same guidelines as any other federal judge.*

BillyM
*small & begrudging? Oh, so Alito.*

QuietMode_MD
*So cringe, really dishonoring the court.*
*But we will lecture everyone else on the appearance of impropriety.*
*"The code is more what you'd call 'guidelines' than actual rules."*
*— Barbossa, Pirates of the Caribbean*

Casie P
*The court is out of control.*

ICarol
*It is empty. It just repeated what they are currently doing with no device for enforcement or correction.*

^•.•^☐⚧murky
*Also has no enforcement for failing to adhere, so it has no teeth. Nothing but a weak attempt by the conservative justices to downplay their corruption.*

Richard W
*It is and will continue to be a fraud institution....*

John S
*I have a feeling they will let improprieties slide. The problem with policing yourself. Need congressional oversight.*

Ms.Bec
*Petty people with large egos*

shep
*The word "imperious" springs to mind for some reason.*

onlinesavant
*It's condescending, and immature of the republicans on the court also. Thinking this meaningless measure is going to get the legislative branch off its constitutionally mandated dictate of oversight of it. Judicial reform will happen in 2025.*

Charles W
*Just DESTROYED their future Rulings.*

Jamie K
*deck chairs - nothing more*

Richard W
*It is and will continue to be a fraud institution....*

CharBar -
*And as it stands it's a Paper Tiger to appease the little people. The Committee on Judiciary needs to pressure SCOTUS to adopt standard overseeing and enforcement processes and forward the bill on 18yr term limit*

Bebop
*Great to have code, but.... It has no teeth.*

John S
*I have a feeling they will let improprieties slide. The problem with policing yourself. Need congressional oversight.*

Ms.Bec
*Petty people with large egos*

momofc
*All this is a CYA to deflect. They have done nothing, and it will not stop the scrutiny that swirls around this corrupt court.*

Gregg L P
*now investigate what they did and took*

iputadollarin
*The absence of a code - Does not mean - There is no code*

Sheryl M
*So many in powerful positions loose their humanity. Or maybe they never had it.*

Mary A
*Small & Begrudging will be the epitaph of this SCOTUS*

VM

*I thought the section about how many free RVs a justice is allowed to be gifted at a time sounds promising if they change a few shoulds to shalls.*

Gordon V 🤍 🤍 🤍 🐾

*Their arrogance and corruption are the stuff guillotines are made on.*

Bob P
@bp_pack

*The Code is worthless without enforcement. It is nothing more than a PR move.*

Just M

*Gaslighting is far too polite for what they've done. They minimize the need and effect of by demeaning the people who objected to their decades of unethical behavior. Whichever Justices wrote/signed off on that entitled BS need to be removed. They are unfit.*

Godot ✺ US UA

*The release of this "code of ethics" is completely and utterly meaningless. The GOP is a party that has decided that the constitution is to be completely ignored. What would any other piece of paper be worth if the constitution is worth nothing?*

Troy

*A small step indeed... A promise. A pinkie-swear.*

April G

*It's an insult to the American people.*

Walther M

*Clarence Thomas' actions were not good behavior and he can be removed from office. The Code is used as an excuse for Congress to do nothing, "well, he didn't know any better" "there was no specific rule against it" when his actions demonstrate he doesn't have necessary judgment.*

Day
*This corrupt & dishonest facade, replete with temper tantrum, is a perfect representation of the Roberts Court: Ego-driven bullies throwing themselves pity parties while abusing the Law for personal profit.*

Max N
*We keep making noise and highlighting their outrageous behavior. With this statement #RobertsCourt is trying to melt back into the darkness. #MakeGoodTrouble*

Charles K 🏴‍☠️
*It's a great big deal of BULLSHIT is what it is.*

Mary P
*The problem is that the Justices are so high on their own fumes that they believe those of us among the great unwashed are going to buy this nonsense.*

Wolf K
*Impeach all and start over*

it'sathing
*NO! It's like taking your reusable bag to the grocery store. BRAVO...you remembered to bring one. Then loading up your groceries and finding out it has an opening at both ends. STUPIDITY RULES. This "ethics code" is merely a placebo to get citizens off of SCOTUS' back. SHAMEFUL*

https://x.com/SenWhitehouse/status/1725243586956996880?s=20
here:
Sheldon Whitehouse
@SenWhitehouse
*Let's take a look at some of the tweaks the Supreme Court made to the lower courts' code of conduct. Swapping out "judge" for "justice" makes perfect sense, but a few of these edits ought to raise eyebrows.*

*Note here the addition of "knowingly."*
*Deleted: "that a judge's conduct contravened this Code, that a judicial employee's conduct contravened this Code, that a judicial employee's conduct contravened the Code of Conduct for Judicial Employees, or that a lawyer violated applicable rules of professional conduct."*
*"Shall" swapped for "should," and "knowingly" sprinkled in a few more times. Setting aside the main problem of no process/no umpires, even the Code itself is watered down for Their Olympian Highnesses.*

Roc Brady United Against Gun Violence
*You know what, Senator Whitehouse? This isn't a code of conduct. It's an intent to betray the public trust and get away with it.*

♡ us ♡ lady4liberty 🌼 UA 🌼
*SCOTUS should be required to follow the same code of ethics required for Federal Judiciary.*

Linne B USIE 🏳️ ☐☐☐☐☐☐NOIL
*Toothless and worthless. Time for hearings and impeachments for justices taking bribes and delivering favorable rulings to their bribers.*

Aunt R
*They know exactly what they're doing, and it says a lot about their lack of honor.*

J in Florida
*Interesting that uses word:*
*"Should" meaning in best interest, but not necessarily gonna happen.*
*VS*
*"Shall" meaning it WILL happen.*
*Wrote many a Procedure for Hospital Care*
*"Should" would have been ripped & I would have been told that I "SHALL" write mandatory rules for Procedures.*

WordSmith
*Their skill building loopholes is on full display.*

TongueofWood
*There is no reason for a separate code. They are Federal judges and should be under the same code as other Federal judges.*

Alyssa in America
*Feeble attempt by the corrupt court to pretend they've adopted ethics.*

# " *Where justice is denied, where poverty is enforced, where ignorance prevails, and where any one class is made to feel that society is an organized conspiracy to oppress, rob and degrade them, neither persons nor property will be safe.*"
# - Frederick Douglass

HERE IS THE SUPREME COURT CODE OF CONDUCT COPIED BELOW. I HAVE ADDED MY COMMENTS [IN BRACKETS].

STATEMENT OF THE COURT REGARDING THE CODE OF CONDUCT

The undersigned Justices are promulgating this Code of Conduct to set out succinctly and gather in one place the ethics rules and principles that guide the conduct of the Members of the Court. For the most part these rules and principles are not new: The Court has long had the equivalent of common law ethics rules, that is, a body of rules derived from a variety of sources, including statutory provisions, the code that applies to other members of the federal judiciary, ethics advisory opinions issued by the Judicial Conference Committee on Codes of Conduct, and historic practice. The absence of a Code, however, has led in recent years to the misunderstanding [THERE IS NO MISUNDERSTANDING. A FEW S.C. JUSTICES HAVE BEEN DANCING WITH CIA CHECCHI FAMILY CORRUPTION. THIS CORRUPTION STAGGERS ON BEING OUT OF CONTROL AND IS HIDDDEN FROM PUBLIC VIEW.] that the Justices of this Court, unlike all other jurists in this country, regard themselves as unrestricted by any ethics rules. To dispel this misunderstanding, we are issuing this Code, which largely [LARGELY = LARGE LIE] represents a codification of principles that we have long regarded as governing our conduct. [OBVIOUSLY NOT TRUE FOR ALL JUSTICES.]

# *"Injustice anywhere is a threat to justice everywhere."* - Martin Luther King Jr.

NOVEMBER 13, 2023

CODE OF CONDUCT FOR JUSTICES OF THE SUPREME COURT OF THE UNITED STATES

CANON 1: A JUSTICE SHOULD [MUST] UPHOLD THE INTEGRITY AND INDEPENDENCE OF THE JUDICIARY.
A Justice of the Supreme Court of the United States should [MUST] maintain and observe high standards of conduct in order to preserve the integrity and independence of the federal judiciary.
CANON 2: A JUSTICE SHOULD [MUST] AVOID IMPROPRIETY AND THE APPEARANCE OF IMPROPRIETY IN ALL ACTIVITIES.
A. RESPECT FOR LAW. A Justice should [MUST] respect and comply with the law and act at all times in a manner that promotes public

confidence in the integrity and impartiality of the judiciary.

B. OUTSIDE INFLUENCE. A Justice should [MUST] not allow family, social, political, financial, or other relationships to influence official conduct or judgment. A Justice should [MUST] neither knowingly lend the prestige of the judicial office to advance the private interests of the Justice or others nor knowingly convey or permit others to convey the impression that they are in a special position to influence the Justice. A Justice should [MUST] not testify voluntarily as a character witness.

C. NONDISCRIMINATORY MEMBERSHIP. A Justice should [MUST] not hold membership in any organization that practices invidious discrimination on the basis of race, sex, religion, or national origin.

CANON 3: A JUSTICE SHOULD [MUST] PERFORM THE DUTIES OF OFFICE FAIRLY, IMPARTIALLY, AND DILIGENTLY.

A. RESPONSIBILITIES.

A Justice should [MUST] not be swayed by partisan interests, public clamor, or fear of criticism. A Justice should [MUST] participate in matters assigned, unless disqualified, and should [MUST] maintain order and decorum in judicial proceedings. A Justice should [MUST] be patient, dignified, respectful, and courteous to all individuals with whom the Justice deals in an official capacity. A Justice should [MUST] not engage in behavior that is harassing, abusive, prejudiced, or biased. A Justice should [MUST] not retaliate against those who report misconduct. A Justice should [MUST] require similar conduct by those subject to the Justice's control. A Justice should [MUST] take appropriate action upon receipt of reliable information indicating the likelihood of misconduct by a Court employee. Except as provided by law or Court rule, a Justice should [MUST] not initiate, permit, or consider ex parte communications or consider other communications concerning a pending or impending matter that are made outside the presence of the parties or their lawyers. If a Justice receives an unauthorized ex parte communication bearing on the substance of the matter, the Justice should [MUST] promptly notify the parties of the subject matter of the communication and allow the parties to respond. A Justice should [MUST] not knowingly make public comment on the merits of a matter pending or impending in any court. The prohibition on public comment on the merits of a matter does not extend to public statements made in the course of the Justice's official duties. For scholarly, informational, or educational purposes, a Justice may describe the issues in a pending or impending case. A Justice should [MUST] require similar restraint by Court personnel subject to the Justice's control. A Justice should [MUST] not direct Court personnel to engage in conduct on the Justice's behalf or as the Justice's representative when that conduct would contravene the Canons if undertaken by the Justice.

B. DISQUALIFICATION.

(1) A Justice is presumed impartial and has an obligation to sit unless disqualified.

(2) A Justice should [MUST] disqualify himself or herself in a proceeding in which the Justice's impartiality might reasonably be questioned, that is, where an unbiased and reasonable person who is aware of all relevant circumstances would doubt that the Justice could fairly discharge his or her duties. Such instances include, but are not limited to, those in which: (a) The Justice has a personal bias or prejudice concerning a party, or personal knowledge of disputed evidentiary facts concerning the proceeding; (b) At a prior stage of the proceeding, the Justice represented a party, or a lawyer with whom the Justice previously practiced law served during such association as a lawyer for a party, or the Justice or lawyer has been a material witness in the proceeding; (c) The Justice knows that the Justice, individually or as a fiduciary, or the Justice's spouse or minor child residing in the Justice's household, has a financial interest in the subject matter in controversy or in a party to the proceeding, or any other interest that could be affected substantially by the outcome of the proceeding; (d) The Justice or the Justice's spouse, or a person related to either within the third degree of relationship, or the spouse of such person, is known by the Justice: (i) to be a party to the proceeding, or an officer, director, or trustee of a party; (ii) to be acting as a lawyer in the proceeding; (iii) to have an interest that could be substantially affected by the outcome of the proceeding; or (iv) likely to be a material witness in the proceeding. (e) The Justice has served in government employment and in that capacity participated as a judge (in a previous judicial position), counsel, advisor, or material witness concerning the proceeding or has expressed during prior government or judicial service an opinion concerning the merits of the particular case in controversy; (f) The Justice's spouse or a person related to the Justice or the Justice's spouse within the third degree of relationship, or the spouse of such person, is known by the Justice: (i) to have served as lead counsel for a party below; or (ii) to be an equity partner

in a law firm that appears before the
Court on behalf of a party to the proceeding and the Court has not received
written assurance that the income from Supreme Court litigation is
permanently excluded from the person's compensation.

(3) The rule of necessity may override the rule of disqualification.

(4) Neither the filing of a brief amicus curiae nor the participation of
counsel for amicus curiae requires a Justice's disqualification.

(5) A Justice should [MUST] keep informed about the Justice's personal
and fiduciary financial interests and make a reasonable effort to keep
informed about the personal financial interests of the Justice's spouse and
minor children residing in the Justice's household. [THE CIA CHECCHI
FAMILY CULT LEADERS ROUTINELY FINANCIALLY
REWARD/FUNNEL BRIBES TO THE ADULT CHILDREN OF
POLITICIANS AND JUDICIAL PROFESSIONALS. THE SUPREME
COURT CODE OF CONDUCT MUST NOT BE LIMITED TO
MINOR CHILDREN. CIA CHECCHI FAMILY CORRUPTION HAS
SEEPED INTO THE LIVES OF ADULT CHILDREN OF JUDICIAL
PROFESSIONALS AS A WAY OF REWARDING CORRUPT
ATTORNEYS, JUDGES, JUSTICES, MILITARY LEADERS, AND
POLITICIANS.]

(6) For the purposes of this section: (a) The degree of relationship is
calculated according to the civil law system; the following relatives are
within the third degree of relationship: parent, child, grandparent,
grandchild, great grandparent, great grandchild, sister, brother, aunt, uncle,
niece, and nephew; the listed relatives include whole and half blood relatives
and most step relatives; (b) "fiduciary" includes such relationships as
executor, administrator, trustee, and guardian; (c) "financial interest" means
ownership of a legal or equitable interest, however small, or a relationship
as director, advisor, or other active participant in the affairs of a party,
except that: (i) Ownership in a mutual or common investment fund that
holds securities is not a "financial interest" in such securities unless the
judge participates in the management of the fund; (ii) An office in an
educational, religious, charitable, fraternal, or civic organization is not a
"financial interest" in securities held by the organization; (iii) The
proprietary interest of a policyholder in a mutual insurance company, or a
depositor in a mutual savings association, or a similar proprietary interest, is
a "financial interest" in the organization only if the outcome of the

proceeding could substantially affect the value of the interest; (iv) Ownership of government securities is a "financial interest" in the issuer only if the outcome of the proceeding could substantially affect the value of the securities. (d) "proceeding" includes pretrial, trial, appellate review, or other stages of litigation.

(7) Notwithstanding the preceding provisions of this Canon, if a Justice would be disqualified because of a financial interest in a party (other than an interest that could be substantially affected by the outcome), disqualification is not required if the Justice (or the Justice's spouse or minor child) divests the interest that provides the grounds for disqualification.

## CANON 4: A JUSTICE MAY ENGAGE IN EXTRAJUDICIAL ACTIVITIES THAT ARE CONSISTENT WITH THE OBLIGATIONS OF THE JUDICIAL OFFICE.

A Justice may engage in extrajudicial activities, including law-related pursuits and civic, charitable, educational, religious, social, financial, fiduciary, and government activities, and may speak, write, lecture, and teach on both law-related and nonlegal subjects. However, a Justice should [MUST] not participate in extrajudicial activities that detract from the dignity of the Justice's office, interfere with the performance of the Justice's official duties, reflect adversely on the Justice's impartiality, lead to frequent disqualification, or violate the limitations set forth below.

A. LAW-RELATED ACTIVITIES.

(1) Speaking, Writing, and Teaching. A Justice may speak, write, lecture, teach, and participate in other activities concerning the law, the legal system, or the administration of justice subject to the following limitations and considerations: (a) A Justice should [MUST] not speak at an event sponsored by or associated with a political party or a campaign for political office. (b) A Justice should [MUST] not speak at or otherwise participate in an event that promotes a commercial product or service, except that a Justice may attend and speak at an event where the Justice's books are available for purchase. (c) A Justice should [MUST] not speak to or participate in a meeting organized by a group if the Justice knows that the group has a substantial financial interest in the outcome of a case that is before the Court or is likely to come before the Court in the near future. (d) A Justice may attend a "fundraising event" of law-related or other nonprofit organizations, but a Justice should [MUST] not knowingly be a speaker, a

guest of honor, or featured on the program of such event.

In general, an event is a "fundraising event" if proceeds from the event exceed its costs or if donations are solicited in connection with the event.

(e) In deciding whether to speak or appear before any group, a Justice should [MUST] consider whether doing so would create an appearance of impropriety in the minds of reasonable members of the public. Except in unusual circumstances, no such appearance will be created when a Justice speaks to a group of students or any other group associated with an educational institution, a bar group, a religious group, or a non-partisan scholarly or cultural group.

(2) Consultation. A Justice may consult with or appear at a public hearing before an executive or legislative body or official: (a) on matters concerning the law, the legal system, or the administration of justice; (b) to the extent it would generally be perceived that a Justice's judicial experience provides special expertise in the area; or (c) when the Justice is acting pro se in a matter involving the Justice or the Justice's interest.

(3) Organizations. A Justice may participate in and serve as a member, officer, director, trustee, or nonlegal advisor of a nonprofit organization devoted to the law, the legal system, or the administration of justice and may assist such an organization in the management and investment of funds. A Justice may make recommendations to public and private fund-granting agencies about projects and programs concerning the law, the legal system, and the administration of justice.

(4) Arbitration and Mediation. A Justice should [MUST] not act as an arbitrator or mediator or otherwise perform judicial functions apart from the Justice's official duties unless authorized by law.

(5) Practice of Law. A Justice should [MUST] not practice law and should [MUST] not serve as a family member's lawyer in any forum. A Justice may, however, act pro se and may, without compensation, give legal advice to and draft or review documents for a member of the Justice's family [CLARIFY IF "FAMILY" MEANS BIOLOGICAL FAMILY OR IF "FAMILY" MEANS SOMEONE WHO IS "LIKE FAMILY," WHICH INCLUDES CLOSE FRIENDS OR MEMBERS OF A FRATERNAL ORGANIZATION, ETC.].

B. CIVIC AND CHARITABLE ACTIVITIES.

A Justice may participate in and serve as an officer, director, trustee, or nonlegal advisor of a nonprofit civic, charitable, educational, religious, or social organization, subject to the following limitations:

(1) A Justice should [MUST] not serve if it is likely that the organization will either be engaged in proceedings that would ordinarily come before the Justice or be regularly engaged in adversary proceedings in any court.

(2) A Justice should [MUST] not give investment advice to such an organization but may serve on its board of directors or trustees even though it has the responsibility for approving investment decisions.

## C. FUNDRAISING.

A Justice may assist nonprofit law-related, civic, charitable, educational, religious, or social organizations in planning fundraising activities and may be listed as an officer, director, or trustee. Use of a Justice's name, position in the organization, and judicial designation on an organization's letter head, including when used for fundraising or soliciting members, is permissible if comparable information and designations are listed for others. Otherwise, a Justice should [MUST] not personally participate in fundraising activities, solicit funds for any organization, or use or knowingly permit the use of the prestige of judicial office for that purpose. A Justice should [MUST] not personally participate in membership solicitation if the solicitation might reasonably be perceived as coercive or is essentially a fundraising mechanism.

## D. FINANCIAL ACTIVITIES.

(1) A Justice may hold and manage investments, including real estate and engage in other remunerative activity, but should [MUST] refrain from financial and business dealings that exploit the judicial position or involve the Justice in frequent transactions or continuing business relationships with lawyers likely to appear before the Court or other persons likely to come before the Court.

(2) A Justice may serve as an officer, director, active partner, manager, advisor, or employee of a business only if the business is closely held and controlled by members of the Justice's family. For this purpose, "members of the Justice's family" means persons related to the Justice or the Justice's spouse within the third degree of relationship as defined in Canon 3B(6)(a), any other relative with whom the Justice or the Justice's spouse maintains a close familial relationship, and the spouse of any of the foregoing.

(3) A Justice should [MUST] comply with the restrictions on acceptance of gifts and the prohibition on solicitation of gifts set forth in the Judicial Conference Regulations on Gifts now in effect. A Justice should [MUST] endeavor to prevent any member of the Justice's family residing in the household [~~RESIDING IN THE HOUSEHOLD~~] from soliciting or accepting a gift except to the extent that a Justice would be permitted to do so by the Judicial Conference Gift Regulations. A "member of the Justice's family" means any relative of a Justice by blood, adoption, or marriage, or any person treated by a Justice as a member of the Justice's family.

(4) A Justice should [MUST] not disclose or use nonpublic information acquired in a judicial capacity for any purpose unrelated to the Justice's official duties.

## E. FIDUCIARY ACTIVITIES.

A Justice may serve as the executor, administrator, trustee, guardian, or other fiduciary only for the estate, trust, or person of a member of the Justice's family as defined in Canon 4D(3). As a family fiduciary a Justice is subject to the following restrictions:

(1) The Justice should [MUST] not serve if it is likely that as a fiduciary the Justice would be engaged in proceedings that would ordinarily come before the Justice or if the estate, trust, or ward becomes involved in adversary proceedings before the Court or in a court under the Court's jurisdiction.

(2) While acting as a fiduciary, a Justice is subject to the same restrictions on financial activities that apply to a Justice in a personal capacity.

## F. GOVERNMENTAL APPOINTMENTS.

A Justice may accept appointment to a governmental committee, commission, or other position only if it is one that concerns the law, the legal system, or the administration of justice, or if appointment of a Justice is authorized by federal law. A Justice should [MUST] not, in any event, accept such an appointment if the Justice's governmental duties would tend to undermine public confidence in the integrity, impartiality, or independence of the judiciary. A Justice may participate in national, state, or local ceremonial occasions or in connection with historical, educational, and cultural activities.

## G. CHAMBERS, RESOURCES, AND STAFF.

A Justice should [MUST] not to any substantial degree use judicial chambers, resources, or staff to engage in activities that do not materially support official functions or other activities permitted under these Canons.

## H. COMPENSATION, REIMBURSEMENT, FINANCIAL REPORTING.

A Justice may accept reasonable compensation and reimbursement of expenses for permitted activities if the source of the payments does not give the appearance of influencing the Justice's official duties or otherwise appear improper. Expense reimbursement should [MUST] be limited to the actual or reasonably estimated costs of travel, food, and lodging reasonably incurred by the Justice and, where appropriate to the occasion, by the Justice's spouse or relative. For some time, all Justices have agreed to comply with the statute governing financial disclosure, and the undersigned Members of the Court each individually reaffirm that commitment.

## CANON 5: A JUSTICE SHOULD [MUST] REFRAIN FROM POLITICAL ACTIVITY.

A Justice should [MUST] not: (1) act as a leader or hold any office in a political organization; (2) make speeches for a political organization or candidate, or publicly endorse or oppose a candidate for public office; or (3) solicit funds for, pay an assessment to, or make a contribution to a political organization or candidate, or attend or purchase a ticket for a dinner or other event sponsored by a political organization or candidate. A Justice should [MUST] resign the judicial office if he or she becomes a candidate in a primary or general election for any office. A Justice should [MUST] not engage in other political activity. This provision does not prevent a Justice from engaging in activities described in Canon 4.

The undersigned Members of the Court subscribe to this Code and the accompanying Commentary.

JOHN G. ROBERTS, JR.

CLARENCE THOMAS

SAMUEL A. ALITO, JR.

SONIA SOTOMAYOR

ELENA KAGAN

NEIL M. GORSUCH

BRETT M. KAVANAUGH

AMY CONEY BARRETT

KETANJI BROWN JACKSON

*" The end of law is not to*
*abolish or restrain, but to*
*preserve and enlarge freedom."*
*- John Locke*

NOVEMBER 13, 2023

Commentary (from Supreme Court Justices)

This Code of Conduct is substantially derived from the Code of Conduct
for U.S. Judges, but adapted to the unique institutional setting of the
Supreme Court. In certain instances, the foregoing Canons provide fairly
specific guidance. A Justice, for example, "should not testify voluntarily as a
character witness." Canon 2B. A Justice "may serve as the executor . . . only
for the estate, trust, or person of a member of the Justice's family." Canon
4E. In many cases, however, these Canons are broadly worded general
principles informing conduct, rather than specific rules requiring no
exercise of judgment or discretion. It is not always clear, for example,
whether particular conduct undermines, promotes, or has no effect on
"public confidence in the integrity and impartiality of the judiciary," Canon
2A, or whether a Justice has acted in a "patient, dignified, respectful, and
courteous" manner, Canon 3A. This concern is heightened with respect to
Canons applicable to Justices of the Supreme Court, given the often sharp
disagreement concerning matters of great import that come before the
Supreme Court. These Canons must be understood in that light.
This Commentary does not adopt the extensive commentary from the
lower court Code, much of which is inapplicable. It instead is tailored to the
Supreme Court's placement at the head of a branch of our tripartite
governmental structure.
Canon 3B addresses the inherently judicial function of recusal. The Justices
follow the same general principles and statutory standards for recusal as
other federal judges, including in the evaluation of motions to recuse made

by parties. But the application of those principles can differ due to the
effect on the Court's processes and the administration of justice in the
event that one or more Members must withdraw from a case. Lower courts
can freely substitute one district or circuit judge for another. The Supreme
Court consists of nine Members who sit together. The loss of even one
Justice may undermine the "fruitful interchange of minds which is
indispensable" to the Court's decision-making process. See Dick v. New
York Life Ins. Co., 359 U.S. 437, 459 (1959) (Frankfurter, J., dissenting).
Recusal can have a "distorting effect upon the certiorari process, requiring
the petitioner to obtain (under our current practice) four votes out of eight
instead of four out of nine." S. Ct. Stmt. of Recusal Policy (Nov. 1, 1993).
When hearing a case on the merits, the loss of one Justice is "effectively the
same as casting a vote against the petitioner. The petitioner needs five votes
to overturn the judgment below, and it makes no difference whether the
needed fifth vote is missing because it has been cast for the other side, or
because it has not been cast at all." Cheney v. United States Dist. Court for
D.C., 541 U.S. 913, 916 (2004) (memorandum of Scalia, J.). And the
absence of one Justice risks the affirmance of a lower court decision by an
evenly divided Court—potentially preventing the Court from providing a
uniform national rule of decision on an important issue. See Microsoft
Corp. v. United States, 530 U.S. 1301, 1303 (2000) (statement of
Rehnquist, C.J.). In short, much can be lost when even one Justice does not
participate in a particular case. This Canon's recusal provisions thus differ
from those in the lower court Code in that they: restate the Justices' 1993
Statement of Recusal Policy; recognize the duty to sit and that the time-
honored rule of necessity may override the rule of disqualification, see
United States v. Will, 449 U.S. 200, 217 (1980) (28 U.S.C. § 455 does not
alter the rule of necessity); ABA Model Code of Judicial Conduct Rule 2.11
cmt. 3 ("The rule of necessity may override the rule of disqualification.");
and omit the remittal procedure of lower court Code Canon 3D. Canon
3B(2)(d) retains language from the lower court Code relating to known
interests of third-degree relatives that might be substantially affected by the
outcome of a proceeding. Because of the broad scope of the cases that
come before the Supreme Court and the nationwide impact of its decisions,
this provision should be construed narrowly. For example, a Justice who
has school-age nieces and nephews need not recuse from a case involving
student loans even though the disposition of that case could substantially

affect the terms on which the Justice's relatives would finance their higher education. The Canon's recusal provisions depend on the Justice's knowledge of certain relationships or interests. The Court receives approximately 5,000 to 6,000 petitions for writs of certiorari each year. Roughly 97 percent of this number may be and are denied at a preliminary stage, without joint discussion among the Justices, as lacking any reasonable prospect of certiorari review. Recusal issues must be considered in light of this reality. In view of the Canon's knowledge requirement and the large volume of cases docketed, the Justices rely on the disclosure statements required under the Court's rules in identifying interested parties that may present grounds for recusal. Individual Justices, rather than the Court, decide recusal issues. See Cheney v. United States Dist. Court for D.C., 540 U.S. 1217 (2004) ("In accordance with its historic practice, the Court refers the motion to recuse in this case to Justice Scalia."). Recusals are noted in the Court's decisions, both at the certiorari and merits stages.

In contrast to the lower courts, where filing of amicus briefs is limited, the Supreme Court receives up to a thousand amicus filings each Term. In some recent instances, more than 100 amicus briefs have been filed in a single case. The Court has adopted a permissive approach to amicus filings, having recently modified its rules to dispense with the prior requirement that amici either obtain the consent of all parties or file a motion seeking leave to submit an amicus brief. In light of the Court's permissive amicus practice, amici and their counsel will not be a basis for an individual Justice to recuse. The courts of appeals follow a similar approach to ameliorating any risk that an amicus filing could precipitate a recusal. Federal Rule of Appellate Procedure 29(a)(2) states that "a court of appeals may prohibit the filing of or may strike an amicus brief that would result in a judge's disqualification." Canon 4 reflects the principle that Justices, like all judges, are encouraged to engage in extrajudicial activities as long as independence and impartiality are not compromised. Justices are uniquely qualified to engage in judicial activities that concern the law, the legal system, and the administration of justice, such as by speaking, writing, teaching, or participating in scholarly research projects. Justices are also encouraged to engage in educational, religious, charitable, fraternal, or civic extracurricular activities not conducted for profit, even when those activities do not relate to the law. Participation in both law-related and other judicial activities helps integrate Justices into their communities and furthers public understanding of and respect for the judicial system.

Canon 4G clarifies that a Justice "should not to any substantial degree use judicial chambers, resources, or staff to engage in activities that do not materially support official functions or other activities permitted under these Canons." This provision recognizes the distinctive security concerns that the Justices face as high-profile public figures and allows the Justices to accept comprehensive security protection. See 40 U.S.C. § 6121(a)(2)(A) (authorizing the Supreme Court Police to protect the Justices when they are not performing official duties). It also allows Court officials and chambers staff to perform their official duties in enhancing security and providing legal, ethics, and other appropriate assistance to the Justices in light of the high public interest in the Justices' activities and the acute security concerns that are distinct from such concerns for lower court judges. And, consistent with historic practice, chambers personnel including law clerks may assist Justices with speeches, law review articles, and other activities described in Canon 4. Canon 4D(3) and 4H articulate the practice formalized in 1991 of individual Justices following the financial disclosure requirements and limitations on gifts, outside earned income, outside employment, and honoraria. Justices file the same annual financial disclosure reports as other federal judges. Those reports disclose, among other things, the Justices' non-governmental income, investments, gifts, and reimbursements from third parties. For purposes of sound judicial administration, the Justices file those reports through the Judicial Conference Committee on Financial Disclosure.

In regard to the financial disclosure requirements relating to teaching and outside earned income, a Justice may not accept compensation for an appearance or a speech, but may be paid for "teaching a course of study at an accredited educational institution or participating in an educational program of any duration that is sponsored by such an institution and is part of its educational offering." 2C Guide to Judicial Policy § 1020.35(b) (2010). Associate Justices must receive prior approval from the Chief Justice to receive compensation for teaching; the Chief Justice must receive prior approval from the Court. See S. Ct. Resolution ¶ 3 (Jan. 18, 1991). Justices may not have outside earned income—including income from teaching—in excess of an annual cap established by statute and regulation. Compensation for writing a book is not subject to the cap. [THE CIA CHECCHI FAMILY CULT LEADERS HAVE FUNNELED MILLIONS OF

DOLLARS TO JUDICIAL, MILITARY, AND POLITICAL LEADERS THROUGH BOOK DEALS IN THE PAST. COMPENSATION FOR WRITING A BOOK SHOULD BE SUBJECTED TO A CAP OR SOME FORM OF REGULATION. ANOTHER FINANCIAL BRIBE TACTIC EMPLOYED BY THE CIA CHECCHI FAMILY CULT LEADERS TO FUNNEL BRIBE MONEY TO MILITARY, POLITICAL, AND JUDICIAL LEADERS INVOLVES PASSING ON INSIDER INFORMATION FOR THE STOCK MARKET. THERE SHOULD BE A BAN ON TRADING STOCKS FOR ALL MILITARY, JUDICIAL, AND POLITICAL LEADERS BECAUSE THE CORRUPTION WITHIN STOCK TRADING HAS BEEN A WELL-ESTABLISHED MECHANISM THAT THE CHECCHI FAMILY CULT LEADERS HAVE ORCHESTRATED FOR MANY DECADES.]

Like lower court judges, Justices engage in extrajudicial activities other than teaching, including speaking, writing, and lecturing on both law-related and non-legal subjects. In fact, the lower court canons encourage public engagement by judicial officers to avoid isolation from the society in which they live and to contribute to the public's understanding of the law. In deciding whether to speak before any group, a Justice should consider whether doing so would create an appearance of impropriety in the minds of reasonable members of the public.

## *"Equal justice under law."*

### - Inscription on the United States Supreme Court Building.

In addition to this Code of Conduct, the Justices also comply with:
• The Constitution of the United States, see, e.g., U.S. Const. Art. I, § 9, cl. 8 (foreign emoluments clause); Amdt. 5 (due process clause).
• Current laws relating to judicial ethics including, but not limited to 28 U.S.C. §§ 455, 2109; the Ethics in Government Act, 5 U.S.C. §§ 13101 – 13111, 13141 – 13145; the Foreign Gifts and Decorations Act, 5 U.S.C. § 7342; Pub. L. 110-402, § 2(b), 122 Stat. 4255; and the Stop Trading on Congressional Knowledge Act of 2012, Pub. L. 112-105, §§ 12, 17, 126 Stat. 303; and
• Current Judicial Conference Regulations on: Gifts; Foreign Gifts and Decorations; Outside Earned Income, Honoraria, and Employment; and Financial Disclosure. See, e.g., S. Ct. Statement on Ethics Principles and

Practices (Apr. 25, 2023).

The Justices may also take guidance from their colleagues, judicial decisions, the Supreme Court's Office of Legal Counsel, the Judicial Conference Committees on Codes of Conduct and Financial Disclosure, lower court judges, executive and legislative branch practice and guidance, state judicial ethics authorities, and from scholars, scholarly treatises, and articles. The Justices also continue to look to the Court's own past resolutions and opinions for guidance. The Court provides mandatory training on judicial ethics principles to all Court employees. In urging the judiciary to promulgate and adopt what became the lower court Code, Justice Tom C. Clark observed shortly after his retirement from the Supreme Court that judges "must bear the primary responsibility for requiring [appropriate] judicial behavior." Hearings on Nonjudicial Activities of Supreme Court Justices and Other Federal Judges before the Subcommittee on Separation of Powers of the Senate Committee on the Judiciary, 91st Cong., 1st Sess., 174 (1969). The same is true for Justices. To assist the Justices in complying with these Canons, the Chief Justice has directed Court officers to undertake an examination of best practices, drawing in part on the experience of other federal and state courts. For example, some district courts and courts of appeals have deployed software to run automated recusal checks on new case filings. The Court will assess whether it needs additional resources in its Clerk's Office or Office of Legal Counsel to perform initial and ongoing review of recusal and other ethics issues. The Court will also consider whether amendments to its rules on the disclosure obligations of parties and counsel may be advisable. In regard to financial disclosure, the Justices will continue to seek guidance from the Office of Legal Counsel and the staff of the relevant Judicial Conference committees, including the Committee on Financial Disclosure, which reviews each Justice's annual filing for compliance with applicable laws and regulations. The Office of Legal Counsel will maintain specific guidance tailored to recurring ethics and financial disclosure issues and will continue to provide annual training on those issues to Justices, chambers staff, and other Court personnel.

## *" The first duty of society is justice."*
## - Alexander Hamilton

*"Formlessness means being so subtle and secret that no one can spy on you. Soundlessness means being so mysteriously swift that no one notices you."*

*A quote from The Art of War, by Master S. Tzu*

# ABOUT THE AUTHOR

Dillon Woods is a multifaceted creative force, intertwining his roles as an author, independent journalist, artist, and musician. His expansive collection of published works is a testament to his diverse storytelling abilities. His passion for exploring the intricacies of life and society is clear in his thought-provoking narratives. His dedication to unearthing unconventional truths and his unwavering commitment to crafting narratives that resonate with depth and meaning render his work undeniably captivating. His heart wrenching accounts of true-life experiences in America make his writing an important addition to America's journalistic landscape, shedding light on poignant realities often overlooked or kept secret. Dillon's ability to articulate fresh and heartfelt stories about real-life experiences in America enriches and elevates the journalistic sphere. His writing serves as a crucial addition to America's journalistic tapestry, offering a genuine and profound portrayal of the human experience – fostering empathy, understanding, and a deeper connection to the diverse fabric of the nation. Explore his writing at www.amazon.com/author/dillonwoods.